D1462141

The Medieval Latin Hymn

The Medieval Latin Hymn

Ruth Ellis Messenger, Ph.D.

Te decet hymnus
Deus in Sion

Psalm 65:1

CAPITAL PRESS
1731 – 14th St., N. W.
WASHINGTON, D. C.

To
J. Vincent Higginson

Contents

Preface

THE PURPOSE of this volume is to trace the history of the medieval Latin hymn from the point of view of usage. It must be evident to any student of a subject which is spread over a thousand years of human experience in the widening environment of an entire continent that a guiding thread is needed to show the way. One must not, at the same time, ignore the fact that a monumental religious literature in the poetic field is involved. But the hymn is functional, having its greatest significance as a lyric when employed in an act of worship. Latin hymnology, moreover, is an aspect of ecclesiastical studies following the history of the Church through the classical and medieval ages into modern times.

A wider cultural background than the immediate interest of theology and religion is reflected in the hymns of any age. Here often lie secrets of interpretation which make possible an appreciation of contemporary thought.

As the study of the medieval hymn is followed from the standpoint of life and usage, the antiquarian and the literary critic, who cannot fully satisfy the quest of the student for reality, must give place to the medieval worshiper himself who has revealed in its entirety each successive phase of a hymnological history not yet ended.

For information about the Christian hymn as it existed prior to the medieval era, the author's *Christian Hymns of the First Three Centuries, Paper IX*, a publication of The Hymn Society of America, may be consulted. This account of primitive Christian hymnody, although premedieval, serves as an introduction to the subject matter of the present volume.

The pages which follow are intended for the general reader rather than the specialist in medieval culture or in the classical languages. Biographies of hymn writers have not been attempted since the literature of this subject is already extensive. Documentation has been reduced to a minimum. A bibliography has been provided for any who are interested in specialized fields.

It is hoped that this brief study will have a modest part in opening up to the general reader a field which has never been fully explored in any language, especially English. An inclusive treatment is not offered here but one which represents the fruits of a generation of research.

My grateful thanks are due to my friends and co-workers in the fields of classical studies, hymnology and medieval history who have assisted me in countless ways, particularly to Dr. Adelaide D. Simpson and Dr. Carl Selmer, both of Hunter College of the City of New York, who have read the entire manuscript and offered invaluable criticisms and suggestions. Among the many librarians who have assisted me in varied centers of study, I am most indebted to the staff of the Library of Union Theological Seminary of New York, under Dr. William Walker Rockwell and later under Dr. Lucy Markley. Finally, I wish to acknowledge my obligation to those authors and publishers who have granted permission to use certain translations of Latin hymns which appear in this volume.

CHAPTER ONE

Early Middle Ages: Latin Hymns of the Fourth Century

I. The Early Hymn Writers

The first mention of Christian Latin hymns by a known author occurs in the writings of St. Jerome who states that Hilary, Bishop of Poitiers (c. 310-366), a noted author of commentaries and theological works, wrote a *Liber Hymnorum.*[1] This collection has never been recovered in its entirety. Hilary's priority as a hymn writer is attested by Isidore of Seville (d. 636) who says:

> Hilary, however, Bishop of Poitiers in Gaul, a man of unusual eloquence, was the first prominent hymn writer.[2]

More important than his prior claim is the motive which actuated him, the defense of the Trinitarian doctrine, to which he was aroused by his controversy with the Arians. A period of four years as an exile in Phrygia for which his theological opponents were responsible, made him familiar with the use of hymns in the oriental church to promote the Arian heresy. Hilary wrested a sword, so to speak, from his adversaries and carried to the west the hymn, now a weapon of the orthodox. His authentic extant hymns, three in number, must have been a part of the *Liber Hymnorum. Ante saecula qui manens,* "O Thou who dost exist before time," is a hymn of seventy verses in honor of the Trinity; *Fefellit saevam verbum factum te, caro,* "The Incarnate Word hath deceived thee (Death)" is an Easter hymn; and *Adae carnis gloriosae,* "In the person of the Heavenly Adam" is a hymn on the theme of the temptation of Jesus.[3] They are ponderous in style and expression and perhaps too lengthy for congregational use since they were destined to be superseded.

In addition to these the hymn *Hymnum dicat turba fratrum,* "Let your hymn be sung, ye faithful," has been most persistently associated with Hilary's name. The earliest text occurs in a seventh century manuscript. It is a metrical version of the life of Jesus in seventy-four lines, written in the same meter as that of *Adae carnis gloriosae.*[4]

Pope Damasus, a Spaniard by birth (c. 304-384), is believed to have written hymns in addition to the *Epigrams* on the martyrs which constitute his authentic poetry. It would seem probable that his activities in identifying and marking the sites associated with the Roman martyrs might have been supplemented by the production of hymns in their honor. Two hymns bearing his name are extant, one in praise of St. Andrew the Apostle and one for St. Agatha. Upon internal evidence the ascription is dubious for they bear the mark of authorship too late to be considered among the poems of this famous Pope.

As a matter of fact, Ambrose, Bishop of Milan (340-397), remains the uncontested originator of the medieval Latin hymn as it becomes familiar to us in a uniform series of metrical stanzas adapted to congregational use. Like Hilary, Ambrose was born in Gaul.[5] He was the son of Ambrose, Prefect of the Gauls, and like his father he attained official appointment under the Roman government as Consular of Liguria and Aemilia, with Milan as place of residence. Theological controversy between the Arians and the orthodox was raging at Milan, the Bishop himself, Auxentius, having adopted the Arian position. Ambrose at this time was a catechumen but at the death of Auxentius was obliged to preserve order when the election of his successor took place. At that very moment the popular mandate created Ambrose Bishop of Milan at the age of thirty-four years. The period immediately following his election found him constantly battling for orthodoxy in a contest which passed beyond the limits of theological debate to the actual siege of orthodox churches by the Arian forces.

Ambrose was acquainted with the Syrian practice of hymn singing, and like Hilary, he recognized the effective use of the hymn by the proponents of the Arian heresy. It was not long before the congregations in the basilica at Milan were chanting antiphonally the praises of the Trinity in a similar form. Ambrose himself recorded his achievement, his biographer Paulinus mentions the event and Augustine in his *Confessions* describes the congregational singing which he himself had heard.

> We, though as yet unmelted by the heat of Thy Spirit, were nevertheless excited by the alarm and tumult of the city. Then it was first instituted that according to the custom of the eastern regions, hymns and psalms should be sung, lest the people should faint through the fatigue of sorrow.[6]

Ambrose wrote hymns appropriate for morning and evening worship, four of which now extant, can be proved to be of his authorship, *Aeterne rerum conditor,* "Maker of all, eternal King," *Deus creator omnium,* "Creator of the earth and sky," *Iam surgit hora tertia,* "Now the third hour draws nigh," and *Veni redemptor gentium,* "Come Redeemer of the earth."[7] Many others in keeping with his style and inspiration have been preserved and subjected to critical study with the result that eighteen hymns on varied themes are generally conceded to be Ambrosian. Had Ambrose never conferred upon the church his gift of hymnody he would still remain one of the great Latin Fathers of the fourth century, in his functions as statesman, organizer and scholar. His contribution to ecclesiastical poetry and music have made him influential century after century. In this role he has spoken directly to multitudes of Christians throughout the world, many of whom have been unacquainted with his name or unaware that they were following the Ambrosian tradition of congregational song.
(See Illustrative Hymns, I. *Splendor paternae gloriae,* "O Splendor of God's glory bright.")

Spain shares the honors with Gaul as the birthplace of the earliest hymn writers, claiming first Damasus and then Prudentius, (348-413?), a lawyer, judge and poet of his era. Little is known of his life aside from his literary work which includes two collections of hymns, the *Cathemerinon,* a series for the hours of the day and the ecclesiastical seasons and the *Peristephanon,* a series of much longer poems in praise of the great martyrs of the early church. In his effort to learn more of the circumstances attending their martrydom, Prudentius went to Rome to visit the scenes made sacred by their death and sufferings. Neither of these collections was written for liturgical use but for devotional reading. Both were destined to be appropriated by compilers of hymnaries, especially in Spain.

Hymns from the *Cathemerinon,* either in their original form or in centos, spread throughout the Christian church while the martyr hymns were also drawn upon but to a lesser extent. The hymns selected for festival use are perhaps most familiar today, for example, for Advent, *Corde natus ex parentis ante mundi exordium,* of which the translation "Of the Father's love begotten," suggests the original meter. The Epiphany hymn, *O sola magnarum urbium,* "Earth hath many a noble city," is also well known.[8]

Considered merely as Latin poetry, the hymns of Hilary, Ambrose and Prudentius are transitional in their literary character. They belong neither to the poetry of the Silver Age of Latin literature nor do they represent the medieval literary tradition. Of the metrical aspect something will be said presently. By some the Ambrosian hymn is regarded as a daring innovation and the model from which vernacular European verse was later to develop. In that case, it constitutes a class by itself. For evidence of the continuity of Latin poetry from the classical to the medieval age we must turn to the *Carmina* of Venantius Fortunatus.

Fortunatus (c. 530-600) was born near Treviso and lived as a youth in northern Italy, studying at Ravenna. The greater part of his life, however, was spent in Gaul which he visited first as a pilgrim to the shrine of St. Martin at Tours, who, he believed, had been instrumental in restoring his eyesight. At Poitiers he met Queen Rhadegunda, wife of Clothair, King of Neustria. She had founded a convent at Poitiers and there lived in retirement. This was his introduction to a life of travel and of intercourse with the great. He was acquainted with bishops, noblemen and kings whose praises he sang in many graceful tributes, occasional poems and epitaphs. Through the influence of Rhadegunda, his lifelong patron and friend, he was ordained, and after her death he became Bishop of Poitiers, 597, where he lived until his death. As a churchman he was an admirer and biographer of the saints of Gaul, preeminently St. Martin whose life and miracles he recounted in poetic form.

Fortunatus seems to have carried with him from the Italian scenes associated with the poetry of Virgil an inspiration which was never entirely lost. His poems suggest a familiarity with the literary background of classical verse. During his mature life he lived in the environment of sixth century Gallic society which was already assuming its medieval

Frankish outlines. Natural beauty and human companionship were alike important to him. He was acquainted with men and women of every degree from the monarch to the slave.

Although the spirit of religious devotion and of orthodox belief is evident in many of the hundreds of lyrics which he composed, four only may be classed as hymns. Three of these are concerned with the theme of the Holy Cross, *Pange lingua, gloriosi proelium certaminis,* "Sing, my tongue, the glorious battle," *Vexilla regis prodeunt,* "The banners of the king advance," and *Crux benedicta nitet,* "Radiant is the blessed cross." The fourth, *Tempora florigero rutilant distincta sereno,* "Season of luminous days, marked bright with the birth of the flowers," is a Resurrection hymn.[9] It is impossible to indicate here the extraordinary influence which this group of hymns has exerted in the evolution of Christian hymnody, continuing in Gaul the tradition, as it were, which Hilary first established. The circumstances of their origin and their lasting values will be considered in connection with processional hymns in Chapter VI.
(See Illustrative Hymns, II. *Vexilla regis prodeunt,* "The banners of the king advance.")

II. Metrical Forms

The problem of metrical forms and the prosody of the earliest Latin hymns, in general, is a phase of the same problem affecting Latin poetry as a whole. The subject is both complicated and obscure, entangled with that of Latin rhetorical prose style, the transition from the quantitative accent of ancient classical poetry to the stress accent of medieval and modern verse and with the origin of rhyme. It is a problem for specialists among whom opinions are now divergent. Toward a practical understanding of the metrical values of the hymns of Hilary, Prudentius, Ambrose and Fortunatus, the pragmatic test of what is singable may be applied. The ancient balanced rhythms of Semitic poetry as illustrated in the Hebrew psalms had been sung for generations. The metrical lyrics of ancient Greece were sung to an instrumental accompaniment as were the Latin lyrics of the Golden Age of Rome. These highly polished classical forms were for the elite. Of popular poetry which was sung in the period immediately preceding the appearance of the Latin hymn, very little is known. The early writers were experimenters. Hilary used classical meters with alterations, of which the trochaic tetrameter catalectic proved most acceptable.[10] It is illustrated in *Adae carnis gloriosae* and also in hymns by Prudentius and Fortunatus. Prudentius used a variety of meters in addition to the trochaic which proved adaptable in actual liturgical practice but by that time stress accent was beginning to obscure the original quantitative values. Ambrose used the unrhymed iambic dimeter, a simple and singable form which has been in vogue ever since, at first unrhymed after the original models and later rhymed. The popular trochaic meter familiarized by Hilary, Prudentius and Fortunatus, when transformed by stress accent and rhyme, is easily recognized both in Latin and the vernaculars. Fortunatus popularized the elegiac meter in hymns for a thousand years by demonstrating its use in *Tempora florigero*. Prior to the ninth century revival of hymnody, the Ambrosian hymn, considered as a metrical model, in comparison with all other existing models, dominates the field equally with its prestige as an expression of Christian theology and devotion.

III. Hymns in Worship

It is evident that the fourth century was one of innovation in the custom of congregational singing as the Ambrosian hymn was more widely diffused. Our knowledge of what actually took place is very incomplete, based first upon the writing of Ambrose and his contemporaries and later upon the hints derived from monastic usage. That morning and evening services of prayer and praise were common is well known. That the singing of the new fourth century hymns was an integral part of such services is largely assumed. Prudentius wrote hymns for the evening ceremony of the *lucernare* or lighting of the candles, a Christian practice adopted from the Greek church, to which many references are found. The fact that the hymns of Prudentius were in existence long before they appeared in the records of formal worship points to early Christian usage, however dimly perceived.

Concerning music we learn from the most recent researches that "nothing definite is known of the melodies that were actually applied to the hymns of St. Ambrose."[11] The traditional liturgical music of Milan is known as the Ambrosian Chant. It cannot be traced to Ambrose himself but is supposed to have existed in a simpler form than that which appears in available manuscripts beginning with the twelfth century. At least it may be said to have existed prior to the Roman Chant and perhaps have influenced the latter. With a frank acknowledgement of ignorance as to the antiphonal melodies which thrilled St. Augustine at Milan, the possibility must be admitted that they reflected to some extent the formal music of the synagogue or the music of the Greeks or the elements of contemporary folk music because these were the musical materials of which the Christians had experience. All three may have been represented, but for a hymn of the Ambrosian type, the chant as evolved in rendering the Gospels or the Psalms may have given place to a form of song more characteristic of the lyric.

IV. Themes

The tradition of Christian hymnology which upholds a way of life is fundamental in Ambrosian and contemporary hymns. The "way" is the first term by which Christianity was designated in the Scriptures. Thus to the Scriptures the hymn writers turned for the living characterization of their themes. The call to a virtuous life is sounded in *Splendor paternae gloriae* quoted above. Similarly throughout these hymns, the high ideal of faith, purity, hope, patience, humility and love and the ethical teachings derived from the words of Jesus and from the early exemplars of the Christian religion are clearly expressed and enjoined. Not alone for contemporaries in a period of crisis and controversy were these hymns effective. They have continued to speak the same words in the same spirit of joy and devotion derived from contact with the earlier springs of faith to every succeeding century.

The writings of men familiar with Roman civilization and trained in classical culture would naturally be presumed to retain the flavor of a non-Christian literature. Christianity had already appropriated from the pagan philosophers those teachings which were congenial to its own. Ambrose reveals both in his poetic and prose writings his acquaintance with classical thought and literary models. Prudentius mingles the classical and the Christian. Fortunatus was inspired by classical poetry to a Christian expression of beauty in form and content. But in every case, these characteristics are marginal. The core of their hymns is the scriptural narrative. Not only is the subject matter faithfully reproduced but the actual text is sometimes embedded in the verse. The result is a rare objectivity and a lack of embellishment especially in the works of Ambrose which became the preferred standard for later writers.[12]

The life of Jesus is a favorite theme particularly in those episodes which were described and expanded in hymns for the Nativity, Epiphany, Passion, Easter and Pentecost. From the episode of the Nativity the praise of the Virgin was developed. The doctrine of the Trinity was everywhere upheld in hymns, even as its defense had been influential in their creation.

The group of hymns which praise the early Christian leaders, either directly or by incidental mention, form a nucleus for the impressive medieval hymnology of the saints. The Apostles have first place both in chronology and importance. Prudentius praised the Roman martyrs and Ambrose those of Rome and Milan as well. Both honored Laurence the Deacon and Agnes the Virgin. To the praise of the whole group "the noble army of martyrs," the hymn *Aeterna Christi munera,* "The eternal gifts of Christ the King," was written, unrivalled as a martyr hymn in any period of Latin hymnology.

(See Illustrative Hymns, III. *Aeterna Christi munera,* "The eternal gifts of Christ the King.")

CHAPTER TWO

Early Middle Ages: The Old Hymnal

I. The Hymn Cycles

We owe the preservation of the earliest Latin hymns to monastic practice. When the founders of monasticism in the west, Caesarius and Aurelian who were famous bishops of Arles (6th C.), and Benedict (d. 543), founder of the Benedictine Order, organized the regulations and routine for the communities under their charge, they incorporated Latin hymns already existing into the daily worship of the monastery.[1] These were sung at the services of the canonical hours and were known as hour hymns or office hymns.

A continuity can be traced, although faintly, from primitive Christian observances. Beginning with the vigil of Saturday night in preparation for the following Sunday, the first three centuries of Christian history developed public services for prayer at candlelight, night time, and dawn. By the fourth century, the tide of devotional practice had set in, bringing with it daily worship in the church at the third, sixth and ninth hours. At the end of the fourth and during the fifth century the cycle was completed with new offices at sunrise and nightfall. The full series, therefore, included the nocturnal cursus; vespers, compline, matins (nocturns and lauds), and the diurnal cursus; prime, terce, sext and nones.[2] An opportunity was afforded to unify the services and at the same time to make use of the symbolic number seven by reference to *Psalm 119: 164 (Ps. 118, Vulgate)*, "Seven times a day do I praise thee because of thy righteous ordinances." From the simple assemblies of early Christianity, therefore, and the daily offices of prayer, a fully elaborated cycle of hymns in time developed, appropriate to the symbolism of the seven hours and to the needs of the annual feasts. Constantly increasing in number and variety, these cycles were preserved in psalters together with the psalms or in a hymnary by themselves. In fact, the word *hymn* came to mean specifically an office hymn later to be associated with the breviary, and the word *hymnal,* a cycle or collection of office hymns.

At first the cycles were brief. Five extant manuscripts reveal the sixth century group of hymns of which the best representative, the so-called Psalter of the Queen from the famous collection of Queen Christine of Sweden, probably dates from the time of Charles Martel (d. 741).[3] This group of hymns is usually referred to as the *Old Hymnal,* the initial version of which numbers thirty-four hymns but at the close of the sixth century had increased to perhaps sixty hymns in actual use.[4] The thirty-four original hymns of the *Old Hymnal* are listed in the Appendix to this chapter where the appropriate location of each is indicated, whether for daily or seasonal worship.

Due to the influence of Benedict who had enjoined the use of the Ambrosian hymn, the authentic verse of Ambrose was preserved and extensively imitated among the regular clergy. What had become of the hymn in secular worship?

The old prejudice against non-scriptural hymns and in favor of the Psalms had never died out. By a canon of the Council of Laodicea (c. 364), *psalmi idiotici* or "private hymns" were forbidden, a mandate which was valid during the lifetime of Ambrose who, nevertheless, ignored a restriction intended to safeguard orthodoxy but hardly applicable in his case. In the sixth century the secular clergy of Spain were forbidden to use hymns by the Council of Braga, 563.[5] The paradox of encouraging non-scriptural hymns in the monastery and forbidding their use in the church at large has been explained by reference to the contemporary appearance of early forms of vernacular speech in western Europe. Latin, the language of the church, its liturgy and its clergy, was now threatened by a possible inroad of the vernacular.[6] Hymn writing was regarded, perhaps, as a prerogative of the clergy to be kept within bounds. To throw open to the church everywhere these privileges might be dangerous alike for theology and worship. Learning in the Latin tongue tended to be concentrated in the monastery, for other centers of scholarship were few and far between; hymnology became largely a function of the monastic group.

It should be remembered that these centuries embraced a period of the greatest political, economic and social confusion in western Europe during which we know relatively little about Christian worship in widespread congregations except for the rite of the mass. Yet in the sixth century the opposite tendency toward greater freedom in writing and singing hymns was apparent. The Council of Tours, 567, permitted the secular clergy to use Ambrosian and other hymns.[7] If viewed in this light, the religious verse of Fortunatus takes on a new significance, illustrative of the freedom which the Church in Gaul, always highly individual, now experienced in the realm of hymnology.

Gaul, then, was the scene of a conflict in which the Latin hymn was contending, and that successfully, for its very life. On the monastic side, anonymous clerics, using the Ambrosian model, gradually provided the full complement of hymns for the annual festivals in harmony with the liturgical year which began to emerge and resemble somewhat its present form. Wherever the Benedictine Order penetrated into the territories of western Europe, the use of hymns likewise increased. Their diffusion must be regarded as comparable with that of an organization which within two hundred years of the death of its founder boasted hundreds of monasteries and convents throughout western Christendom, augmented by Irish and other foundations which had adopted the Benedictine Rule. Missionary zeal had played a significant role in this expansion. Fulda, for instance, a community with 400 monks and many missionaries at its disposal, was able under Willibald to extend its influence through numerous subordinate monasteries and convents. Royal favor, already enjoyed by St. Gall and now conferred upon new establishments, rivalled that of popes and synods, which at the time of Pippin's coronation in 750 or 752, combined to insure the success of the Benedictine program.[8]

On the side of secular worship, the hymnal used by Benedict and his successors gradually gained a foothold in the church through diocesan centers which adopted the monastic cycles. Or perhaps it may be said, with the reservation that we are in the realm of theory and not of fact, that the ancient hymns written prior to the sixth century had been circulated and continued to be circulated in the west in a way not at present understood, in connection with the Gallican or ancient liturgy of Gaul. If so, the *Old*

Hymnal is the Gallican hymnal which Benedict appropriated and his followers maintained to its acknowledged prestige by the year 750.

An episode of significance for hymnology during the period under consideration in this chapter is the activity of Gregory the Great who occupied the papal throne from 590 to 604. A member of the Benedictine Order, he is noted for his enthusiastic support of its missionary program and for his interest in ecclesiastical music and poetry. His role in the extension of the Roman Rite and of the Benedictine Order to Britain is familiar to all.[9] His authority in the western church is a matter not of controversy but of fact. That he was deeply interested both in hymn writing and singing may be safely assumed for there are too many reports of his activity to be ignored. His actual role in the development of the chant which bears his name and the authorship of eight to eleven hymns attributed to him, have not been determined. For Gregory's contribution to the ritual music of the church the reader is referred to the discussion of this subject by specialists in the field of liturgical music. For his contribution to the hymn cycles, modern hymnologists have judged even the eight hymns singled out as Gregorian by Benedictine editors, to be doubtful although the nocturn and vesper hymns may be authentic.[10] Aside from critical research the fact remains that all these hymns appear in the cycles of the day and several have been in liturgical use to the present time. They are representative of the hymnology of the transition between the *Old Hymnal* and the later cycles whose hidden origins Gregory may have influenced.
(See Illustrative Hymns, IV. *Nocte surgentes vigilemus omnes,* "Father we praise Thee, now the night is over.")

II. Mozarabic Contributions

The list of hymns in the *Old Hymnal* (See Appendix) reveals at a glance the presence of nine Mozarabic hymns. Mozarabic is a term applied to the Christian inhabitants of Spain under Moslem rule and also to the rites of the Christian Church prevailing throughout the Visigothic and Moslem periods. It is the former or Visigothic period extending from the foundation of the Kingdom by Euric, 466, to the entry of the Moslems in 711, which claims our attention here. Connections between Spain and Gaul at this time were very close for the Visigoths ruled a large part of what is now southern France from the Atlantic to the Maritime Alps. The great churchmen of Spain, especially Isidore, Archbishop of Seville (d. 636), performed the same service for Christian hymns in Spain which the monastic leaders performed in Gaul. In his *Etymologiae* and his *De officiis ecclesiasticis,* Isidore considers the subject of music and liturgy. His *Regula monachorum,* built partly on older rules observed in Spain, is an evidence of his interest in monastic reform. As presiding bishop of the IV Council of Toledo, 633, he was at the height of his reputation.[11] Braulio, Bishop of Saragossa, (631-651), his pupil and literary executor, bears witness to his fame.[12] He himself maintained the liturgical tradition which was continued with great success by Eugenius II, Primate of Toledo, (646-657), Ildefonsus who held the same rank, (659-667), and others. As the result of the literary and liturgical movement initiated by these leaders, supported by the councils and schools, the Mozarabic hymnology was rapidly developed. The canons of the IV Council of Toledo, for which Isidore may have been personally responsible, require uniformity of the rites and offices throughout Spain and Gaul. The thirteenth canon upholds the validity and appropriateness of hymns by Christian authors against those who would restrict the hymnody of the Church to the Psalms of the Old Testament. After a discussion of the old prohibitions and the reasons for approving the new compositions, Canon 13 reads:

> "As with prayers, so also with hymns written for the praise of God, let no one of you disapprove of them but publish them abroad both in Gaul and Spain. Let those be punished with excommunication who have ventured to repudiate hymns."[13]

Building upon the work of Ambrose, Sedulius and notably Prudentius, their own countryman; adapting ancient traditions of congregational worship and monastic usage, the liturgists of the seventh century must have collated for the use of the clergy approximately sixty-five hymns from sources originating prior to their own day. These ancient hymns form the nucleus of the Mozarabic Hymnal, the earliest manuscript of which dates from the tenth century. They reveal interrelations between the Spanish and Gallican churches and they indicate a continuity of hymn singing from

primitive congregational usage like the Ambrosian to the seventh century revival and extension of non-scriptural hymns.[14]
(See Illustrative Hymns, V. *Alleluia piis edite laudibus,* "Sing alleluia forth in duteous praise.")

III. Celtic Hymns

The Celtic inhabitants of the British Isles from the period of the introduction of Christianity maintained individual features of liturgy and organization, especially in their monastic groups. The contemporary Saxon Church of the seventh century, however, had been drawn into the Roman sphere of influence by Gregory the Great who was also in touch with Celtic leadership. The ancient record of the interchange of hymns written respectively by St. Columba of Iona and by Gregory preserves more than a report incapable of proof.[15] It points to reciprocal interest in the evolving hymnology of the sixth and seventh centuries in Celtic and continental regions.

The so-called Bangor Antiphonary of the seventh century is the earliest manuscript containing hymns, twelve in number.[16] Its contents are otherwise miscellaneous, including a list of the abbots of Bangor. Hilary's supposed hymn from this collection, *Hymnum dicat turba fratrum,* has already been cited. An ancient communion hymn, *Sancti venite Christi corpus sumite,* "Draw nigh and take the body of the Lord," is included and *Mediae noctis tempus est,* "It is the midnight hour," an office hymn common to the hymnals of Spain and Gaul. Among other important sources is the Irish *Liber hymnorum,* preserved in an eleventh century manuscript of Dublin which contains Columba's hymn, *Altus prosator,* "Ancient of days," honoring God the creator, and the *Lorica* or *Breastplate Hymn* of St. Gildas (6th C.), *Suffragare trinitatis unitas, unitatis miserere trinitas,* "Grant me thy favor, Three in One, have mercy on me, One in Three."[17]

On the whole Celtic hymns exhibit great variety in subject matter and purpose with many departures from the type of hymn cycle in use on the continent. Indeed, the group of from fifteen to twenty hymns produced in the centuries under consideration are highly distinctive. The Ambrosian tradition is not apparent. Non-Ambrosian meters are illustrated in all three hymns cited above while alliteration, the *abcd* form, repetition of initial words and other metrical devices are found throughout the collection. There are hymns for the offices and communion, metrical prayers and a group of hymns for saints, some bearing witness to local cults. Poetic individuality marks them all.[18] Contemporaneous with the flowering of Celtic hymnology, the seventh century saw the beginning of the cultural invasion of the continent by Celtic scholars, teachers and missionaries whereby two streams of culture, previously isolated, united with significant results for the hymnology of the future.

(See Illustrative Hymns, VI. *Sancti venite Christi corpus sumite,* "Draw nigh and take the body of the Lord.")

IV. Summary

The account of the Christian hymns of necessity accompanies that of the Christian organization, moving from the shores of the Mediterranean and the Christian centers in Roman provincial areas into the "regions beyond" of missionary effort. Although congregational singing in the Ambrosian sense appears to have been submerged in this process, the traditional hymnody was preserved, new hymns added and the foundation laid for the ninth century revival.

Anonymity is the rule and known authorship the exception for the hymns produced in the fifth, sixth, seventh and eighth centuries. This continued to be the rule during the whole medieval period since the names of those who wrote the non-scriptural parts of religious rites were lost or unknown or perhaps of little importance in communal worship. The fact that the hymns which survive have been gathered from liturgical manuscripts and not from the work of individual authors except in rare cases, should make anonymity more intelligible.

Hymn sources are scanty and interconnections, dimly perceived, can rarely be established. Continuity of evolution is often broken or replaced by new poetical inspiration. However, the fourth century appeal to the objective, the direct, the simple, is seldom varied by the subjective theme. The biblical narratives and the symbolism connected with the various offices and feasts add substance and character to the cycles and to the concept of the liturgical year.

In the heart of the Dark Ages, popularly considered, western European civilization was in confusion and its fate problematical. One could scarcely expect the fruits of peace and security to flourish. Yet in these very centuries there were created and circulated many of the best loved hymns of Christianity, a number of which have been in unbroken use to the present day. Among them are the illustrations inserted above and *Lucis Creator optime,* "O blest creator of the light;" the Advent hymns, *Verbum supernum prodiens,* "High Word of God who once didst come," and *Conditor alme siderum,* "Creator of the stars of night;" the Easter hymn, *Claro paschali gaudio,* "That Easter day with joy was bright;" for the dedication of a church, *Urbs beata Jerusalem,* "Blessed city, heavenly Salem" with the more familiar second part, "Christ is made the sure foundation." Two hymns honoring the Virgin date from this period: *Ave maris stella,* "Hail, Sea-Star we name Thee," and *Quem terra pontus aethera,* "The God whom earth and sea and sky," initiating the Marian hymnology of the Middles Ages.[19]

("See Illustrative Hymns, VII. *Ave maris stella,* "Hail, Sea-Star we name Thee.")

Created and preserved in a clerical and for the most part a monastic environment these hymns express the Christian thought and faith of the era which was thus treasured up for wider circulation and influence in a later and more settled society. The words of the late Canon Douglas, a great American hymnologist, are memorable in this connection:

> "What does have a practical bearing on our subject is, that whatever may have been the older cycle, it was enriched to an extraordinary degree in the early medieval centuries. What began in Milan, and achieved its permanent recognition at Monte Cassino, was soon to bring about a Mozarabic Hymnal in Spain, a Gallican hymnal in northern Europe, an Anglo-Irish cycle in Britain: and from all these various increments not only enlarged the growing Hymnal but also richly diversified it."[20]

Appendix

Old Hymnal (*See Anal. Hymn., 51, Introduction* p. xx).

Ad nocturnas horas

Mediae noctis tempus est (Mozarabic; in Bangor Antiphonary)

Rex aeterne Domine

Magna et mirabilia

Aeterne rerum conditor

Tempus noctis surgentibus

Ad matutinas laudes

Deus qui caeli lumen es

Splendor paternae gloriae

Aeternae lucis conditor (Mozarabic)

Fulgentis auctor aetheris (Mozarabic)

Deus aeterni luminis (Mozarabic)

Christe caeli Domine

Diei luce reddita

Ad parvas horas

Postmatutinis laudibus

Certum tenentes ordinem (Mozarabic)

Dicamus laudes Domino (Mozarabic)

Perfectum trinum numerum (Mozarabic)

Ad vesperas

Deus creator omnium

Deus qui certis legibus (Mozarabic)

Deus qui claro lumine

Sator princepsque temporum

Ad completorium

Christe qui lux est et dies (Mozarabic)

Christe precamur adnue

Proprii de tempore

Intende qui regis

Illuminans altissimus

Dei fide qua vivimus

Meridie orandum est

Sic ter quaternis trahitur

Hic est dies verus Dei

Iam surgit hora tertia

Iam sexta sensim volvitur

Ter hora trina volvitur

Ad cenam agni providi

Aurora lucis rutilat

De communi martyrum

Aeterna Christi munera

CHAPTER THREE

The Ninth Century Revival: Hymns

I. Background of Carolingian Culture

To explain fully the origin of a great literary movement must always be difficult, for the subtle influences affecting its beginnings elude a scientific analysis of facts. One observes the revival of Latin hymnology between 750 and 900 A.D. with amazement. The voices of Ambrose, his contemporaries and his immediate imitators had been silenced for centuries. Venantius Fortunatus had stood forth, a solitary survival of the old Latin poetic genius or, perhaps more accurately, a solitary herald of the new medieval awakening. Then a flowering of religious poetry spread over western Europe, not to be withered by new barbarian invasions but to be the permanent possession of the Christian Church.

In this period the older cycles of office hymns were revised and expanded and fresh cycles created in such numbers as to justify the new terminology of the *Later Hymnal* or *Ninth Century Hymnal*. The sequence arose in the formal worship of the mass, affording a new inspirational to clerical poets and resulting in a body of sacred verse of increasing influence. The processional hymn and its related forms appeared in response to the new impulse toward a hymnic accompaniment to ceremonial acts. In effect, the hymn during the period under consideration, was well established in every aspect of formal worship.

In the background of the age which created this literature must be sought the trends and motivation which make intelligible the voices of its interpreters. Accordingly, in the years from 750 to 900 A.D. when the Carolingian rulers, Pippin, Charlemagne, Louis the Pious and Charles the Bald were guiding the destinies of the Franks, the various influences affecting public worship must be surveyed. The most important were the liturgical reforms undertaken or sponsored by the Carolingian rulers; their promotion of ecclesiastical music and singing; their interest in the reform and expansion of the Benedictine Order; the literary activity of members of the Carolingian court circles who devoted themselves to liturgical studies or poetic expression; the part played by Celtic culture; the infiltration of Byzantine ideas and arts and the rise of Germanic genius.

The introduction and permanent establishment of the Roman liturgy in Frankish realms form the background of public worship in the Carolingian era. When Pippin ascended the throne in 752, the Gallican Rite prevailed. When the reign of Charles the Bald came to a close in 877, the Roman Rite was supreme.[1] Charlemagne received the Gregorian Sacramentary from Pope Hadrian I.[2] Stimulated by his desire to unify the Germanic peoples under papal as well as imperial authority, he brought about by royal edicts or capitularies a widespread reform in the western continental church. Those features of his program which affected hymnology include requirements that priests must be educated, that monks observe their monastic rule, that the singing of the psalms and the *gloria* be improved, that schools of singing and grammar be founded in monastic and diocesan centers, that both regular and secular clergy be urged to acquire knowledge and skill in singing, that the Roman Chant be ordained, that a singing school be established at Aix-la-Chapelle, that the clergy read and sing well.[3] Charlemagne's successors, Louis the Pious and Charles the Bald continued his reforming policy.

In the legislation cited above, Charlemagne had followed his father's example which favored a training in Gregorian music under Roman teachers, as developed in the schools of Rome.[4] Pippin's interest had resulted in the establishment of a musical center of great repute at Metz[5] which also possessed a cathedral school representative of the finest institutions which flourished at this time side by side with monastic centers of learning.

Charlemagne was presented with a copy of the Benedictine Rule with choir rules, office and festival hymns, by Theodomar, Abbot of Monte Cassino, sometime between 787 and 797.[6] It became his chosen duty to promulgate the Rule, to require its observance everywhere within his realms and further to extend the influence of the Order in general. Consequently, monastic centers of music arose, for example, at St. Gall where the hymnody of the offices was fostered and gradually made available for the bishoprics as well. Louis the Pious, (814-840), and Charles the Bald, (843-877), in their turn continued the patronage of the Benedictine Order. Already fortified by the efforts of Charlemagne, the Benedictines entered a period of religious and cultural influence which was later merged into the age of the universities. Linked directly with the program for monastic reform, the impulse to write new hymns and the encouragement to finer musical performance together created the annual cycles of this period in which the older hymns were retained and supplemented by the new.

The writers and literary leaders of the Carolingian period were by virtue of their clerical profession actively engaged in liturgical studies. Alcuin compiled the missal which established the Gregorian Sacramentary in Frankish realms and constituted a recension acceptable to the Roman Church.[7] A significant innovation for hymnology was the decorative procession.[8] Alcuin was also influential through his devotional works which supplemented the public worship of the mass and offices. Paulus Diaconus and Angilbert were second to Alcuin in promoting liturgical studies. The works of the great writers were accompanied by numerous writings of lesser importance which bear witness, as will be evident below, to the increasing practice of hymn-singing. The influence of the Roman Rite, largely barren of hymns, was at the same period, in contact with the influence of Benedictine precedent in hymn singing which in the end prevailed.

The Latin poetry associated with the Carolingian era has been edited and published in a monumental form under the title *Poetae Latini Aevi Carolini*.[9] The collection, produced in the spirit of a classical revival by a circle of court poets, includes secular as well as religious verse.

Carolingian culture not only in the specific field of literature but in the broader sense afforded a medium for the spread of Celtic, Byzantine and Germanic genius. The Celtic portion of the poetry in the early monastic cycles has already been described in connection with the *Old Hymnal*. Prior to the eighth century, a transfer of Celtic scholarship to the continent began to take place. The missionaries, Columbanus, Gall, Foilan, Disibod and others, came first, during the seventh and eighth centuries. Refugees, fleeing before the Norse invasions of the late eighth and ninth centuries, followed. Wanderers and pilgrims crossed the Channel, among them *peregrini* who left their homeland to live in new countries as a means of spiritual satisfaction and reward. Scholars came also who hoped for a more sympathetic reception for their teachings among the continentals.[10] On the whole, Celtic immigrants found a welcome. Charlemagne himself favored them.[11] Celtic teachers were proficient in orthography, grammar, Greek, scriptural and liturgical subjects and the arts.[12] They brought with them manuscripts, the influence of which was felt, not only in their subject matter but in musical notation and characteristic scripts.[13] The Bangor Antiphonary, the hymns of which have already been considered, came to the continent at this time. Among the famous teachers of music was Marcellus[14] who, at St. Gall, instructed Notker, Tutilo, Waltram and Hartmann, a fraternity devoted to finer ecclesiastical music and hymnody.

The role of Byzantine influence cannot be ignored in any account of the cultural and historical background of ninth century literature. One should recall that the Carolingian period was an era of general European intercourse which could not fail to have an effect upon society. The foreign relations of the Frankish Empire necessitated much traveling, visiting and correspondence. Warlike as well as peaceful movement, commercial or cultural, increased the interchange of ideas. There was an overlapping of boundary lines, too, which amalgated populations. The infiltration of Byzantine influence might be conceived as a by-product of European intercourse.

Insofar as hymnology is concerned, musical contacts between the Byzantine and Frankish realms were frequent. As early as Pippin's reign, Byzantine musicians appeared at the Frankish court with a gift of an organ from the Emperor Constantinus Copronymus.[15] Many refugee monks who fled to the west during the iconclastic controversy remained there even after its close in 787, enjoying monastic hospitality and imperial favor. Charlemagne permitted them to use the Greek language in worship and was so much impressed by the music employed in chanting the psalms that he caused it to be adopted for the Latin version also.[16] The paramount influence of Byzantine music upon liturgical practice in the west will be considered more fully in connection with the sequence.

Verifiable traces of Byzantine influence had already appeared with the activities of Gregory the Great and are entirely comprehensible, so far as he is concerned, in view of his residence at Constantinople, 579-585, as papal envoy of Pelagius II.[17] The importation of litanies into the west illustrates this type of influence. When Charlemagne received the Sacramentary from Pope Hadrian I, it was labelled "Gregorian." But in the interval between the lives of Gregory and Charlemagne, popes of eastern origin, ruling at the end of the seventh and the beginning of the eighth century were responsible for western practice.[18] The influence of the Eastern upon the Western Church seems to have been cumulative, with Charlemagne in his day acting as the agent for its diffusion throughout the Frankish Church.

In matters concerning the church and its worship the Greeks were an acquisition not only as musicians but as scholars and as experts in the fine arts. Their scholarship was in demand in New Testament studies. Illustrations of Greek and of oriental inspiration in general are numerous in architecture, painting, sculpture, ivories, work in precious metals and the decoration of manuscripts.[19] Perhaps it was a natural desire to emulate the splendor and ornament of eastern rites which led Charlemagne to favor Greek elements in western observance at the expense of the Gallican.

In the midst of Gallic, Celtic, Italian, Byzantine and oriental influences mingled in Carolingian culture, the presence of native genius is strongly felt. Charlemagne has been criticized for his devotion to classical rather than Germanic culture. Sacred poetry as produced in the Carolingian literary circles, was written in Latin and clothed in classical garb. It could hardly have been otherwise since Latin was demanded by the Church and the vernacular languages of western Europe were then in their early infancy. But in spite of the studied artificiality of this verse, a note is sometimes heard in harmony with the poetry of later centuries which emanates from Germanic sources.

Such in brief is the background of that revival of hymnody which appears in the Carolingian period. It remains to trace, in detail, the evolution of the monastic hymnal known as the *Later* or *Ninth Century Hymnal*.

II. The Later Hymnal

The enlargement and diversification of the Hymnal to which Canon Douglas referred in the words quoted at the close of Chapter Two, occurred within the general historical limits of the Carolingian era and with the exception of Spain and the British Isles, within the general geographical limits of Carolingian political influence. The hymn cycles of the period, recorded in manuscripts which reflect the numerical increase in hymns as well as their diffusion upon the continent, are associated with religious centers, for example, St. Martial, Laon, Douai, Moissac, St. Germain-des-Prés, Corbie, Jumieges, Reichenau, Treves, Schäftlarn near Munich, Murbach, Rheinau, St. Gall, Einsiedeln, Bobbio, Monte Cassino, Benevento, Padua, Toledo, Canterbury, Naples and many other places. The nucleus of the *Later Hymnal* has been identified with the hymn cycle found partly in a *hymnarium* of the ninth century from St. Paul's in Lavantthal, Carinthia, and partly in a similar manuscript from Karlsruh, both manuscripts being associated with Reichenau.[20] The basic hymns from this group of sources current in the Carolingian period are listed in the appendix to this chapter. A complete list of the manuscript sources (prior to 1100), including the above and others, with an index of the hymns which they contain, approximately 800 in number, was provided by James Mearns, the English hymnologist, in his *Early Latin Hymnaries.*[21]

So much for the evidence as to the actual hymns in use from sources available at the period when the *Later Hymnal* flourished. The origin of the *Later Hymnal,* however, is far from clear. It has been defined as a collection arising about the seventh century which superseded the *Old Hymnal* and has since prevailed.[22] This opinion advanced by Blume and affirmed by Walpole, depends upon the theory that the later cycle had been in use in the British Isles since the period of Gregory the Great. An Anglo-Irish cycle therefore, was posited which took possession of the continent, usurping the original Benedictine hymnal. As early as 1911, Blume's theory was questioned by Wilmart, the Benedictine scholar, who asserted that the early cycle constituted a Gallican hymnal only,—a possibility mentioned above. He thought that the *Later Hymnal* was a new version of the Benedictine cycle representing a normal growth through the centuries. Other critics of note have adopted one or the other viewpoint, Frere following that of Blume; and Raby, that of Wilmart.[23] A final solution is obviously impossible for lack of manuscript evidence.

At the accession of Charlemagne, 768, the future of liturgical hymnody was uncertain as the forces of Roman usage and Benedictine practice were in conflict and the possibility of transferring the Benedictine heritage to the church extremely doubtful, as the preceding survey has already made clear. Secondary forces, however, were at work to achieve this very end. First, the early gains made in compiling the Gallican Hymnal and extending it to the secular clergy were never entirely lost. A precedent had been set. Second, the Benedictine cycle was enjoined wherever the Rule was effective and its use was further stimulatd by royal capitularies upon the subject of music and singing. Third, the establishment of monastic centers of music in the leading Benedictine abbeys was productive of literary as well as musical effort, attested by the very manuscripts of hymn collections gathered there. The manuscripts of St. Gall, for example, cover every department of contemporary medieval hymnology.

Charlemagne was particularly interested in St. Gall but was also concerned with the monastic centers at Mainz, Fulda, Treves, Cologne, Bamberg, Hersfeld, Lorsch, Würzburg and Reichenau.[24] He founded Neustadt and endowed twelve monasteries in Germany. Meanwhile missionary zeal had guided Benedictine pioneers beyond the old boundaries, and Bavaria and Frisia had already been opened to missions and incidentally to the full round of Benedictine activities. Louis the Pious was active in monastic reform through his association with Benedict of Aniane; he was a special patron of St. Gall and he stimulated the efforts of leaders from Corbie to found New Corbie. Charles the Bald was a benefactor of Marchiennes, Compiègne, Prum and St. Denis.[25] Prior to this period, the numerous and influential foundations established on the continent by Irish monks had adopted the Benedictine Rule, swelling the total number of centers devoted to religious and educational activities.

The numerical increase in the Benedictine abbeys offers in itself presumptive evidence of a greater use of hymns. What is known of the monastic centers and their store of hymnaries offers direct proof. A closer bond between the Order and the cultural activities of the age is found in the great personalities drawn from Benedictine ranks to serve the imperial designs. Of particular interest here are the statements regarding hymns and hymn singing which appear in contemporary writings.

Alcuin was chiefly interested in the Roman liturgy as such but he wrote *De psalmorum usu, Officia per ferias* and the *Epistolae,* the last of which shows a special interest in music. Rabanus Maurus testifies to the general use of hymns by secular as well as regular clergy. Amalarius of Metz mentions the use of hymns outside the monasteries. Walafrid Strabo traces the use of hymns from the time of Ambrose and repeats the Canon of Toledo recommending hymns. He says that churches which do not use hymns are exceptional.[26] The testimony is scattered but it points to the adoption of the hymnal by the secular clergy. It should also be recalled that the Ambrosian tradition of musical independence was constantly maintained at Milan.

As the Latin language became more and more an exclusive clerical possession, the old safeguards provided by monastic walls were no longer necessary. The whole body of clergy whether regular or secular became the custodians of the hymnaries used in monastic and diocesan centers of music and scholarship.[27] The Christian laity of Europe at this period may have been largely ignorant of their hymnic heritage because the Carolingian extension of hymn writing and hymn singing occurred within clerical ranks. There was at this time scant indication of the future course of Latin hymnology which would ultimately restore to the layman his original possession handed down from the Early Christian Church.

The poetical writings of the era included a substantial body of religious verse from which hymns are attributed to the following authors: Paulus Diaconus, 1; Paulinus of Aquileia, 7; Alcuin, 3; Theodulphus, 1; Rabanus Maurus, 2; Walafrid Strabo, 5; Florus of Lyons, 2; Wandelbert of Prum, 1; Paulus Albarus of Cordova, 1; Cyprian and Samson, 2; Sedulius Scottus, 2; Milo, 2; Ratbod, 2; Hucbald, 1; Hartmann, 4; Ratpert, 4; Eugenius Vulgarius, 1; these with 73 of doubtful authorship make a total contribution of 114 hymns.

(See Illustrative Hymns, VIII. *Ut queant laxis resonare fibris,* "In flowing measures worthily to sing," Paulus Diaconus.)

Ambrosian meters are set aside in favor of the classical meters of the

Greeks, the Sapphic and elegiac meters proving to be the most popular thereafter. To what extent this influence is actually observable in hymn cycles may be determined by a comparison of the list of Carolingian hymns with the lists of hymns provided by Blume, Julian or Mearns. Batiffol selected thirteen as found in later breviary lists[28] but the actual direct contribution is much larger if other than breviary hymns are admitted. Moreover, the literary and liturgical studies of the time broadened the original Benedictine concept that the hymns of the monastic cycle should be Ambrosian in style. The hymns of Sedulius and particularly of Prudentius and Fortunatus were recognized, introduced or freely adapted to ecclesiastical usage.

The direct influence of Celtic culture upon the new hymn cycles must be associated with the introduction of biblical and liturgical works containing hymns into Frankish territory. Later, hymns were written by Celtic scholars, for instance, Samson, Sedulius Scottus (enumerated above) and possibly others who are anonymous. Blume's theory of the Anglo-Irish hymn cycle, originally sponsored by Gregory the Great and finally transferred to the continent, illustrates the most decisive form which Celtic influence has so far been presumed to have exerted. The list of hymns (see Appendix) bears, on the contrary, no resemblance to the group of contemporary Celtic hymns.[29] It seems much more probable that Gregory, the Benedictine Pope, approved the use in Anglo-Irish lands, of the continental hymn cycle which the Order was responsible for carrying northward with it when it entered Britain. In any case, the Benedictine cycles from the ninth century onward are enriched from every aspect of the diverse culture of the age, in which the Celtic contribution, both direct and indirect, is important.

At this period hymnology in the Greek-speaking world was at its height. Yet proof is sought in vain that Greek hymns were used in the west, either in the Greek language or in translation. The hymnal of the Western Church received from Greek sources its recorded tunes, not its words. Although the earliest liturgical manuscript with musical notation dates from the ninth century, the Greeks had already given their neumes to the west. As for the hymn melodies which are crystallized in these manuscripts when they do appear, theories of origin abound. A definite system of notation was in existence from the seventh century but hymns had been sung from the fourth century.

In modern times through the consecrated efforts of Benedictine students of the chant, working chiefly at Solesmes, a collation of the existing musical manuscripts produced in the Middle Ages, has been made. Their object has been to determine the authentic melodies of the Benedictine cycle throughout its long history. Today the results of their scholarship are available to the public and the great hymns which they have fostered may be heard as well as read in their medieval form.

The assimilation by the Franks, of alien cultures whether through conquest or peaceful interchange, may have been to a certain extent inevitable and involuntary. Such phenomena occur in every period of history. It is the conscious appropriation by the Carolingian leaders of a cultural heritage and its organization through existing institutions which reveals their true genius. This same process had taken place when Roman genius secured and conserved the achievement of the Greeks. In the field of religious culture with which this volume is concerned, an unbroken continuity had been maintained from the days of the primitive church. Even in the minor category of Christian hymnology, the hymnal as such, created in the fourth century, was to flourish all the way into our own times and might have done so without any special intervention. Historically speaking, in the ninth century and under Frankish auspices, a transformation took place which must be attributed to the conscious effort of Frankish churchmen who, receiving the old hymnology, restored it to formal worship with a much larger content and a greatly diversified form. Herein lies the fundamental contribution of Germanic genius to the *Later Hymnal*.

Individual hymn writers of the Carolingian age have been named above as far as they are known, of whom Theodulphus of Orleans, Rabanus Maurus and Walafrid Strabo are perhaps the most notable.

A Goth by race, a Spaniard by birth, Theodulphus, (c. 760-c. 821), belonged to that population dwelling north and south of the Pyrenees which the Franks had amalgamated into their kingdom. He was learned in all the wisdom of that age and a man of action in a sense understandable in any age. Bishop of Orleans, courtier, officer in the administration of

Charlemagne, he served the church and the state with equal distinction. Theodulphus as a poet of sacred verse is best known for his Palm Sunday processional hymn, *Gloria, laus et honor tibi sit,* "All glory, laud and honor,"[30] which he wrote during the period of his fall from royal favor under Louis the Pious. This beautiful processional hymn, a triumph of Carolingian verse, invested with all the attraction of legend and religious pageantry, has been a favorite in every period of Christian history. Theodulphus was not a member of the regular clergy and he did not, as far as we know, write hymns for the monastic cycle. He represents the contemporary trend which brought the hymn into new areas of worship in the offices and ceremonies of the cathedral.

Rabanus Maurus, (780-856), of Germanic origin, was primarily a theologian. His boyhood studies were completed at Fulda. As a young man he became a pupil of Alcuin at Tours. In his maturity he returned to Fulda reaching the climax of his career as Abbot of Fulda and later, as Archbishop of Mainz. As a writer, Rabanus undertook to hand on, through excerpts, the knowledge of his predecessors. He wrote commentaries on the Bible, discussed ecclesiastical organization and discipline, theology, liturgy and worship and the liberal arts. He made translations into German with the collaboration of Walafrid and a Latin-German glossary for the Scriptures. In connection with worship he became interested in the Latin hymns which were rapidly spreading through the west. He discussed the Psalms as hymns and then the hymns of Hilary and Ambrose, saying of the Ambrosian hymns, how widespread had become their prestige in his day. We know from other evidence that he was acquainted also with the hymns of Sedulius, Columba and Bede. It seems almost certain that he practiced the art of poetry although we are restricted to a very small remnant of verse conceded to be his. The poems include a number of hymns for the festivals of the seasons and of the saints, illustrating the vogue for the classic in metrical forms. Like Theodulphus, he wrote for processional ceremonies. The Pentecostal hymn, *Veni, creator spiritus,* has been persistently associated with the name of Rabanus but without adequate proof. It is a lasting hymn of the ninth century.

(See Illustrative Hymns, IX. *Veni, creator spiritus,* "Creator-Spirit, all-Divine.")

Walafrid Strabo, (809-c. 849), was like Rabanus of Germanic origin and like him a member of the regular clergy. At Reichenau he received his early education and at Fulda his theological training under Rabanus. Walafrid was drawn into the courtly circle of Louis the Pious whose son Charles he tutored and whose wife Judith became his literary patron. His life was one of scholarship, prosperity and contentment almost to the end of his career. Louis had appointed him Abbot of Reichenau, a place dear to him from boyhood. From these happy surroundings and from his garden which he immortalized in careful and loving description, he was ousted during the civil conflict following the death of the emperor. At the end he was restored to Reichenau and there he died. His hymns like those of Theodulphus and Rabanus, although few in number, were written in the spirit of the classical revival. Some were intended for festivals and others which will be described in connection with processional hymnody, were written to honor royal patrons.

In reviewing the basic hymns of the *Later Hymnal* (see Appendix), one finds only two of Mozarabic origin whereas nine were duplicated in the *Old Hymnal* in Spain and Gaul. The new cycles in areas under Frankish influence appear to diverge from the Mozarabic as they become more diversified. At the same time, Mozarabic sources reveal a parallel evolution of the hymnal in the Iberian peninsula. The existing manuscripts were collated and edited in 1897 by Blume in volume twenty-seven of the *Analecta Hymnica* under the title *Hymnodia Gotica,* comprising 312 hymns of which 210 were identified by him as Mozarabic in origin.

The hymns of Spain, first assembled under the auspices of Gothic churchmen as recounted in Chapter Two, continued to increase with the encouragement and participation of Mozarabic liturgists, scholars and prelates. The generation that supported Isidore of Seville was succeeded two hundred years later by the group associated with Eulogius, Archbishop of Cordova (d. 859), who fostered the old traditions under Moslem control.[31] In spite of a ruling power alien in every aspect of culture, Christian hymnology held its own. After the Moorish invasions, it is estimated that between thirty and forty hymns were written, several of which contain references to the yoke of the oppressor and petitions for its removal.[32] When the movement toward the expulsion of the Moors had been successfully

initiated and the Roman Rite introduced (1089) the Mozarabic hymnals were comparable to the finest of the continental cycles. In certain instances the contacts between Spain and Gaul were close and direct even under the rule of the Moslems. Theodulphus of Orleans combined the Gothic and Carolingian trends. Alcuin was indebted to Mozarabic sources in his reform of the Frankish rites.[33] Hymns of Mozarabic origin appeared in other parts of western Europe and vice versa.
(See Illustrative Hymns, X. *Deus immensa trinitas,* "O glorious immensity.")

The possible influence of Arabian music and poetry upon the Christian hymn has been a tempting idea and one most elusive of pursuit. Studies of medieval Spanish music and musical instruments have failed to demonstrate that the ecclesiastical chant in Spain was thereby affected. Such novelties as it may have possessed have been traced to influences similar to those which had long before affected the Ambrosian chant and been transmitted to the west. As for the tentative assumption that Arabian lyric poetry influenced contemporary hymn writers in Spain, the evidence narrows to the mono-rhyme or repeated end-rhyme common to Arabian poetry and to several Mozarabic hymns.[34] The whole subject of the Arabian impact, highly controversial as it is, appears to be concerned with influences, which when scrutinized, are observed to spring from cultures prior both to Christianity and to Islam.

The Mozarabic Hymnal in its fully developed version possessed an unusually large number of hymns honoring local saints. This feature must be referred to the history of the Roman persecution in the Iberian peninsula where the complete destruction of the Church was intended and martrydom was the rule. Again the Hymnal is unique in its hymns for public occasions either of mourning and intercession in time of war, pestilence, drought and flood or of joy, in festivals of the consecration of bishops, the coronation of kings and thanksgiving for full harvests.

III. Characteristics

For the most part the hymn writers of the later hymn cycles are anonymous, like their predecessors in this field. Anonymity is then the first characteristic to be noted concerning the hymnal in this period, which makes it necessary to survey the whole as an objective achievement of the age, not of a few individuals.

Next to the anonymity of its authorship, possibly the most conspicuous feature of the new hymnal is the enlargement of each of its general divisions, the Common and the Proper of the Season and the Common and the Proper of Saints. The old hymn cycle, it will be recalled, comprised thirty-four hymns as listed by Blume. The later cycle in its nucleus numbers thirty-seven hymns of which seven are repeated from the old cycle. In ten representative tenth century hymnals, the hymns number from about fifty to about one hundred, many of them common to several lists.[35]

Not only is the total number of hymns increased but festival hymns are multiplied, the ecclesiastical year as it was later known being fully established in hymnology. Advent, Nativity, Epiphany, Lent, the Passion, Easter, Ascension, Pentecost and Trinity have their own groups of hymns. The various feasts of the Virgin and that of All Saints are honored. Among the Apostles, Sts. Peter, John and Andrew are praised; of other biblical saints, Sts. John the Baptist, Stephen, Paul; of the angels, St. Michael; of martyrs, the Innocents and St. Laurence; of local saints, Sts. Martin of Tours, Gall, Germanus, Martial, and a number of others. So stands the record of manuscripts of the tenth century when hymnal gains had been consolidated. The process went steadily onward as Latin hymns for the offices continued to be written to the end of the Middle Ages. A few have been added since the sixteenth century but, with certain exceptions, the great body of office hymns of the medieval church was permanently established by 1100, the date which Mearns selected as a boundary line. The same sources enriched the present-day Roman breviary which by a paradox of history, has preserved to modern times the representative hymns to which the Roman liturgy of that early period was so inhospitable.

As a matter of fact, in the interval between and including the fourth and the eleventh centuries, the Latin hymn, considered in its literary implications and in its liturgical usage, was founded for the ages. Attaching to the word *hymn* its strictest sense and narrowest function, that of the office hymn, the student perceives the great significance of this department of medieval hymnology as compared with the sequence, processional and extra-liturgical hymns of the Middle Ages. It becomes more evident that here is the core and heart of Latin hymnody. The Church could and did in the event, dispense with much of its medieval collection, but never with the hymnal. Here was preserved the ethics of the Christian life, the intimacy of the scriptural narrative, the presentment of the Christian feasts and the praise of God and of his saints.

Appendix

Later Hymnal (See *Anal. Hymn., 51, Introduction* p. xx-xxi)

Ad parvas horas

Iam lucis orto sidere
Nunc sancte nobis spiritus
Rector potens verax Deus
Rerum Deus tenax vigor

Ad vesperas

Lucis creator optime
Immense caeli conditor
Telluris ingens conditor
Caeli Deus sanctissime
Magnae Deus potentiae
Plasmator hominis Deus
Deus creator omnium (In Old Hymnal)
O lux beata trinitas (Mozarabic)

Ad nocturnas horas

Primo dierum omnium
Somno refectis artubus
Consors paterni luminis
Rerum creator optime
Nox atra rerum contegit
Tu trinitatis unitas
Summae Deus clementiae

Ad matutinas laudes

Aeterne rerum conditor (In Old Hymnal)
Splendor paternae gloriae (In Old Hymnal)

Ales diei nuntius

Nox et tenebrae et nubila

Lux ecce surgit aurea

Aeterna caeli gloria

Aurora iam spargit polum

Ad completorium

Christe qui lux es et dies (In Old Hymnal; Mozarabic)

Te lucis ante terminum

Proprii de tempore

Ad cenam agni providi (In Old Hymnal)

Aurora lucis rutilat (In Old Hymnal)

De communi sanctorum

Martyr Dei qui unicum

Rex gloriose martyrum

Aeterna Christi munera (In Old Hymnal)

Sanctorum meritis inclita gaudia

Virginis proles opifexque

Iesu corona virginum

Summe confessor sacer

CHAPTER FOUR

The Ninth Century Revival: Sequences

1. Origin

The problem presented by the origin of the sequence is perhaps the most difficult of all those connected with the evolution of medieval hymnology. So far the available information on the subject has never been brought together in one place. To do so is a baffling task which has by no means been completed here nor is that which follows either exhaustive or conclusive. It is merely an attempt to trace the origin and early development as far as the evidence at hand makes it possible, at the same time referring the reader to those scholars who have investigated special topics in detail.

The *alleluia* of the mass is the starting-point of the sequence. Inherited from the synagogue and incorporated in the Byzantine rite, it was nevertheless brought independently to Rome. The extension of the final *a* constituted a musical phrase, called a *iubilus* or *iubilatio*. This elaborated *alleluia* with *iubilus* is Gregorian.[1] It became necessary for the sake of breathing, to divide the extended *iubilus* into musical phrases, each a *sequentia* and the whole *sequentiae*. Some *iubili* however, remained single while others were sung by two choirs with a repetition of phrases. The next step was the composition of a text for some of the *iubili,* which text was written below the musical notation. Finally a text was supplied for every such melody, which resulted in the *sequentia cum prosa*.[2]

It is one thing to note the preceding succession of steps as objective phenomena. It is quite another to explain the origin of the idea which transformed the *alleluia* into the larger *iubilus*. This is the most obscure point in the musical development of the sequence, which, for lack of manuscript evidence cannot at present be clarified. At least three hypotheses have been offered. Arguing from the appearance of the trope, some have suggested that the *iubilus* is a musical interpolation just as the trope is a textual interpolation. This is quite possible but perhaps too simple for an adequate solution. A much more tempting hypothesis has appealed to a variety of scholars, – that of the introduction of Greek melodies.[3] To these students it has seemed more than probable that the intercourse between western Europe and the Byzantine realms in the reign of Charlemagne constitutes a sufficient explanation for the appearance of fresh musical themes. Again, a possibility only has been suggested. So far manuscript evidence for the Greek melodies from which the Gregorian *alleluiae* and their *iubili* are derived, has not appeared. Blume, whose treatment of the subject forms the basis of this chapter, not only questions the hypothesis of Greek melodies but he offers a third suggestion and that tentatively; Gregory, he thinks, shortened the *alleluia* brought over by the Greeks. When, later, a tendency was felt to elaborate the forms of worship, the longer melodies were once more revived in the sequence. This very interesting suggestion, if one day capable of proof, would harmonize the Byzantine and Gregorian influences which produced the initial extension of the final *a* of the *alleluia*.

For purposes of clearness a differentiation should be made between the musical and poetical development of the sequence as soon as the *sequentia cum prosa* is reached. Manifestly it is impossible to do so, in any complete fashion, where words and music are so inextricably interwoven in a common development. It is better, however, to attempt the impossible and for the present, to ignore overlappings.[4]

The origin of the word *sequentia* itself, in the phrase *sequentia cum prosa* has often been discussed because of its significance in tracing the musical development of the forms in question. To some scholars *sequentia* means merely *sequela, i.e.* notes following the *a* of the *alleluia,* a simple and tenable theory. To the great majority, however, *sequentia* is a translation of the Greek *akoulouthia.* In fact it has been generally accepted as such, although *sequentia* conveys the idea of continuation in the Greek word rather than its technical meaning of a continuation specifically of songs, etc. If this is valid, Greek influence upon the origin of the sequence is inferred.[5] Another form of the theory of Greek influence is evident in the suggestion that *sequentia* means *hirmos,* that is, a regular continuation of tones. *Hirmos* may refer to poetry also.[6] A derivation of *sequentia* from Greek terms, if proven, would of course, buttress the theory of Byzantine influence upon the whole development; but the weakness of the derivation from *akoulouthia,* for example, is its dependence upon a misunderstanding of the Greek form of worship to which the word applies.[7] An entirely different suggestion as to origin arises from the formula used in the liturgy to announce the Gospel, *Sequentia Sancti Evangelii secundum etc.*[8] Often some practical consideration, extraneous condition or unrelated incidental circumstance has affected liturgical change or development. Consequently, even a slight suggestion like this provokes thought.

Whatever may be the correct origin of the word *sequentia* the place of origin of the sequence is generally conceded to have been France sometime in the eighth century. The part played by other lands in the origin of the *sequentia cum prosa* cannot be wholly determined at present. It must suffice to study the evidence available. It has been demonstrated how the early French sequences have a closer tie with the *alleluia* and how the word is sometimes retained to introduce the *prosae* which accompany the music. There is considerable evidence supporting French priority over the Germans in the creation of these new musical forms, the chief centers of composition being St. Martial, Luxeuil, Fleury-sur-Loire, and Moissac, the outstanding rival of St. Martial. An origin for the sequence in France is independently probable due to the interest in liturgical music stimulated by Charlemagne, who, as shown in the preceding chapter, favored Gregorian and Byzantine innovations at the expense of Gallican forms.

One of the suggestions mentioned to account for the original lengthening of the *alleluia* in the *iubilus* is connected with the trope. The word has long been defined as a textual interpolation.[9] Gastoué, however, contends that it was originally and primarily musical, a vocalization in the existing chant and that it was created in the music school. The ancient form of trope is a *neuma triplex* added to the response *In medio etc.* for the Feast of St. John the Apostle, or to *Descendit de caelis* for Christmas. This vocalism is described by Amalarius of Metz and indeed Metz may be its place of origin. Alcuin has been named as the possible originator, a theory strengthened by the fact that Amalarius was one of his pupils.[10] At any rate Amalarius seems to have been the first to call the melody following the *alleluia,* a *sequentia,*[11] from which it is evident that the *iubili* must have been regarded in some other light prior to his writing. The *sequentia* in connection with the *alleluia* may very reasonably have been considered a trope, since vocalisms like these had already appeared elsewhere in rites of worship, and sequences in addition to those which belong to the *alleluia* of the mass have been found in antiphonaries. To repeat, Gastoué describes a musical interpolation or trope originating in the music schools of the Franks and appearing in various liturgical settings. He likens the *iubilus* to a trope which Amalarius called a *sequentia.* The original divisions created by the musical phrases in the *iubilus* now appear in a series, each repeated a certain number of times with introduction and conclusion and thus the completed sequence structure comes into being. The germ of its formal construction, Gastoué finds in certain Gregorian sources. The ancient *alleluia, Justus ut palma florebit,* shows such characteristics and reveals the liturgical Latin origin of the sequence, its melody going back to the *versus alleluiaticus.*

In spite of the evidence which would make the sequence a native musical product of western Europe, the theory of Greek origin is still persistently held by certain scholars. For that reason it must be considered in greater detail. Gregory's adoption of Greek novelties forms the starting point of this theory, while Charlemagne's well-known enthusiasm for Greek innovations carries its proponents still further. The fact that the original Greek melodies which are assumed to have been used in the west, have never been produced in evidence, is not a proof of their non-existence. An extensive study of certain sequence melodies has been made in order to determine whether they are modeled upon Greek originals, since the Greek names for these melodies and features of notation point to such an origin.[12] But such names are secondary, the original and natural name being the first phrase of the Latin words accompanying the melodies and the Greek word a suggested title. A Greek melody, called *Organa,* for instance, might be assumed to retain its name in Latin. The opposite is the case for the name *Filia matris* is original and *Organa* the suggested title.

Regarding the argument from notation it is a matter of common knowledge that the *neume* is native to Greek-speaking lands and may have existed as early as the sixth century.[13] *Neumes* took firm root at St. Gall, the great German center for the propagation of the sequence, so much so, that they persisted until the twelfth century even after the invention of the staff and in the interval were spread by teaching. Moreover, *neumes* were written in the manner of the eastern church, *i.e.* in a straight line, not at different levels to indicate pitch.[14] It is unfortunate that the dearth of manuscripts showing *neumes* makes a gap in the evidence just where support is most needed, for the earliest musical manuscripts with this notation date from the ninth century;[15] but the assumption in favor of Greek originals is at least strong enough to forbid its being ignored.

An additional circumstance which supports the theory of Greek origin is the fact of musical parallelism in the structure of the sequence. This is an important point of contact between the sequence and Byzantine musical forms, although it has not been universally convincing. On the contrary, some have traced this phenomenon of musical parallelism to one of those extraneous conditions, affecting liturgical practice, namely, the use of antiphonal choirs.[16]

Nothing can be more unsatisfactory to the student who is trying to force the sequence into any particular theory of musical origin than the contemplation of what is actually known on this subject, for the question seems destined to remain undecided. A better perspective may be reached by examining the poetical development of the sequence which began with the *sequentia cum prosa* and ended in a new form of Latin hymn for which melodies were in turn composed.

The text written below the *alleluia* melody is generally accepted as of French origin and likewise the naming of that text. As the text became important the melody too was named so that the melody and text were differentiated from each other, the latter as a *prosa*. It is unknown whether the name *sequentia* instead of *prosa* was chosen deliberately as differing from the French usage. Amalarius was apparently the first to use the word *sequentia* in connection with the music. Later the term was destined to supersede the name *prosa* for the poetical text.

We owe to Notker, whose part in creating the sequence will be considered in greater detail below, an account of his invention of words as an aid to memorizing the elaborate melody of the *alleluia* trope. Whether Notker was the first to see the value of this device and to employ it, is unknown.[17] As a theory of origin it has always been popular, being held by Frere and many others. For the present it may be acknowledged that it is a reasonable theory for, of course, only the choir leader had a musical codex to refer to and the musical ability of the average monk was unequal to the difficulties of memorization by ear alone. Moreover, this theory can always be accepted with others, althrough it seems inadequate by itself.

A second explanation of origin arises from the possibility that sequence poetry originated in the imitation of Greek hymn models. The statement has been made definitely that sequence poetry shows the transference of the Byzantine structure of hymnody to Latin church poetry, especially Notker's.[18] With every circumstance favoring such a transfer it is amazing that the Franks who heard so much of Greek hymns and could have translated them into Latin and sung them to the same tunes, evidently did nothing of the kind. Some other explanation of similarity must be found. Metrical parallelism, which is characteristic of the Latin sequence and contemporary Greek hymns, in Gastoué's opinion, can be accounted for only by reference to Hebrew poetry as the ultimate inspiration of liturgical poetry.[19] Thus a Byzantine theory of origin breaks down when metrical sources are subjected to closer scrutiny. After all, the sequence is unknown in the Byzantine ritual and therefore the Byzantine influence could never have been direct.

A third theory emphasizes the metrical form of the *alleluia* melody as the determining factor in creating a new poetical rhythm.[20] Here, the desire to create fitting expressions of praise is not explained so much as the form in which the praises are cast. Von Winterfeld thought that rhythmical prose was inseparable from the liturgical music which had already been composed, just as the Greek chorus and the Wagnerian music drama found their complement in a dignified and sonorous prose rhythm.[21] This theory may well be called the liturgical. It is most significant for the lyrical movement in general since a new metrical form is created differing from the Ambrosian meter or the revived classical meters popular among Carolingian poets. The lyric is born again, as Meyer expresses it, in the music of the church.[22] A poem arises consisting of a series of parallel strophes with introduction and conclusion, a lyric counterpart to the musical phrases of the *sequentia*.

II. Sequences of the German School

The importance played by St. Gall in the development of the sequence has given rise to the theory that it originated there. Present-day opinion, as indicated above, concedes that sequences arose in France and that St. Gall is not a place of origin but like St. Martial, a prominent center for their composition and diffusion. Other centers were Metz, Murbach, Fulda, Echternach, Kremünster and St. Florian. Reichenau, too, was important in music and in the spread of sequence poetry.[23]

Notker Balbulus, (840?-912), was largely responsible for the enviable reputation enjoyed by St. Gall. Born in Switzerland, Notker had entered the Benedictine monastery at St. Gall as a child to be educated and there he continued as a member of the Order until his death. A pupil and later a teacher of the music school in the period of Louis the Pious and Louis the German, he shared the life of the Abbey during the height of its reputation, when its doors were open to travelers from every land and every rank of society. Notker himself tells of the refugee from the French monastery of Jumièges who brought with him his famous Antiphonary. Tradition has it that Notker composed words to fit the forms of the *alleluia-iubilus,* note for note, already in use in his monastery, and thus originated the sequence, finding his inspiration, not in the Ambrosian hymns but in the liturgy.[24] The Jumièges Antiphonary reached St. Gall about 860, by which time *prosae* were already known in France. There is evidence, moreover, from manuscripts, that texts existed before Notker's time in St. Gall. He is not their first composer nor are the sequences emanating from St. Gall necessarily all Notker's work. "Notkerian" means for sequences what "Ambrosian" means for hymns.

The problem of the authentic Notkerian sequences was subjected to critical study and variously solved by Schubiger in 1858, Wilmanns in 1872, and Werner in 1901. More recent students have re-examined the evidence and expressed their critical opinions as to Notker's poetical and musical prestige: Singer in 1922, Van Doren in 1925 and Clark in 1926. Of more than 100 sequences attributed to Notker, 47 were judged to be authentic and edited in volume 53 of the *Analecta Hymnica.* Notker's ability as a musician appears to be a matter of controversy. A new review of the Notkerian problem and its literature has been offered by the Swiss scholar, Wolfram von den Steinen, together with an edition of the sequences of the St. Gall school.[25] What scholars in general have taken away from Notker with one hand they return with the other, for if not an originator he is conceded to be the leading agent in introducing the sequence into Germany and setting a standard for this type of poetry which included from Notker's pen a notable group of sequences for the festivals of the whole year. His sequence for Pentecost is representative of the achievements of the German school.

(See Illustrative Hymns, XI. *Sancti spiritus adsit nobis gratia,* "The grace of the Holy Ghost be present with us.")

It is not surprising that scholars interested in the theory of Greek influence upon sequence poetry should seek confirmation of their views in Notker's work. There is a majestic quality and a vigorous resounding praise in these poems which has been thought a reflection of Byzantine hymns. Reference has already been made to the Byzantine strophic system and its probable influence upon Notker's poetical technique. When one considers that the monastery of St. Gall was always a port of call for refugees and travelers from the east and in the preceding century may have harbored many of them, it is reasonable to suppose that Notker was acquainted with contemporary Greek hymnody. Whatever may be the explanation of the metrical system employed by Notker, he undoubtedly named his melodies in such a way as to suggest a Greek identification.[26]

There remains another line of research, which relatively unimportant, yet should be noted when the question of Greek influence is raised. It has been stated that Greek words are used in Latin sequences, thereby proving contact with Greek-speaking contemporaries on the part of their authors, or with Greek literary sources. Whenever this test is applied to any medieval writing produced by churchmen it should not be forgotten that the Vulgate was the one great continuous source, inspiration and standard of the Latin language as employed in the Middle Ages. Throughout the period, all Latin hymns which include a narrative element or refer in any other way to biblical statements are greatly indebted to the Vulgate. A considerable number of Greek words, naturally, appear in the Vulgate. Applying the criterion of Greek words to Notker's sequences, one reaches no definitive results whatever. In the forty-one sequences attributed to Notker by Wilmanns, some seven Greek words appear which are not in the Vulgate.[27] If this proves anything in Notker's case, it is significant only in connection with other evidence from Greek originals which has not been advanced.

Having considered the separate development of the musical and poetical aspects of the sequence, as far as they can be sundered, it remains to view certain factors which may have affected that development but have not as yet been stated.

The history of medieval music, quite apart from the creation of the *iubilus* and the *sequentia,* should not be overlooked by the student who is trying to understand liturgical music in this general period. Perhaps during the eighth and certainly from the ninth century, polyphonic and harmonic forms began to appear. New melodies for sequences were in demand and were produced, which in turn were influenced by popular and secular music, with an interaction of words and music taking place, sometimes with words, sometimes with music leading the way.[28] The history of the sequence, when complete, will owe much to the studies of medieval music now in progress by musicologists, some of whose conclusions have been noted above. The history of musical instruments is relevant here but in any case it must always be remembered that the church possessed the musical notation and was able to dominate the field.

If the course of secular and ecclesiastical music accompanying the sequence remains uncertain, so are the currents of medieval religious and secular verse in Latin still uncharted. Which is the original stream? Latin secular poetry existed contemporary with the early sequence, the secular form of which was known as a *modus,*[29] which, like the sequence, was inseparable from its musical accompaniment for the minstrel both sang and played his unrhymed lay. Some have taken the extreme point of view of the part played by secular influence and have regarded the sequence as a popular lyric in worship, perhaps even a *Volkslied.*[30] But the question as to the predominance of influence whether religious or secular, remains open.

The argument for influence from vernacular verse upon the sequence is equally weak. Prior to the ninth century vernacular lyrics in the Germanic tongues are so rare as to be valueless in this discussion. Celtic lyrics from the seventh and eighth centuries are also rare. It is possible that they were known to Celtic teachers on the continent but too much should not be assumed from this possibility or from the fact that the oldest form of Celtic lyric exhibits rhythmic parallelism.[31] French, Spanish and early English vernacular lyrics appear too late to be significant in the problem of origins. In any case, the question hinges upon metrical technique which can be adequately explained without recourse to vernacular lyrics, which, insofar as they do exist, may be regarded as themselves imitations of earlier Latin forms.

The evidence offered by secular lyrics, Latin or vernacular, in the early Middles Ages points to an outstanding growth from the sequence rather than a creative source for the sequence. As a matter of fact the sequence breaks away from the church and itself becomes secular, as the history of poetry in the later Middle Ages bears witness.

The above presentation of what is known as to the origin of the sequence can scarcely be satisfactory to the scientific historian of medieval culture. Full of inconvenient gaps and baffling inconsistencies the evidence remains totally inadequate. One conclusion alone may be advanced and that tentatively; the sequence appears to have been created wholly within the liturgy of the mass. The *troparium* or *tropary,* later the gradual and missal contained the sequences for the annual feasts just as the *hymnarium* or *hymnary,* later the breviary had contained the hymn cycles of the offices.

The appearance of the sequence in the history of medieval hymnody was an episode of the greatest importance not only in the evolution of Latin religious and secular poetry but in their vernacular counterparts. In order to understand the extraordinary popularity and wide diffusion of the sequence it must be emphasized that it is not just another hymn, but an ornament to the mass, individually created for each and every festival with a particular theme in mind. The seasons of Advent, Nativity, the Passion, Easter, Ascension, Pentecost, Trinity, the Virgin festivals of the Nativity, Annunciation, Visitation, Purification and Assumption, the feasts of the Apostles and other biblical Saints, the Martyrs, Confessors and Virgins formed a great series which challenged the finest efforts of the clerical poets. Herein lies the essential interest of this hymnody. The original Latin hymn was associated with daily secular worship and then with the canonical hours of the monastery. The sequence was associated with the celebration of the divine sacrifice.

As a closing illustration for this chapter the Alleluiatic sequence has been selected. Based upon the canticle, *Benedicite omnia opera,* and often attributed to Notker, this superb sequence reaches a height of expression comparable to the noblest hymns of the ninth century revival.
(See Illustrative Hymns, XII. *Cantemus cuncti melodum nunc Alleluia,* "The strain upraise of joy and praise.")

CHAPTER FIVE

Late Middle Ages: Hymns and Sequences

BEGINNING WITH the twelfth century the large number of new hymns and sequences produced point to a degree of creative activity that continued through the High Middle Ages. A recent historian of medieval literature, De Ghellinck, sees the religious poetry of the twelfth century rivalling the secular, and points out that ten thousand specimens of every type of religious verse, from 1060 to 1220, are edited in the *Analecta Hymnica*.[1] Maurice Hélin, whose attractive volume is available in English translation, considers the poetic product of the twelfth century the peak of Latin poetry and "its most original contribution to the intellectual patrimony of the west."[2]

It is easier to repeat such a statement than to present acceptably the relevant evidence in the field with which this chapter is concerned. One might expect a larger proportion of known authors but anonymity remains the rule. The exceptions command recognition among the most notable writers of hymns and sequences in any period of their production.

I. SEQUENCES OF THE FRENCH SCHOOL

The sequence, originally a product of France, already perfected as a poetical form by Notker and the German school of ecclesiastical hymn writers, attained a greater influence and popularity under Adam of St. Victor. In 1130 Adam entered the Augustinian Abbey of St. Victor on the outskirts of Paris and there he remained until his death. Whether a native of France or England is unknown. Like Notker, he followed in his poetic themes the annual festivals. To him have been attributed more than 100 sequences which appear in the manuscripts of St. Victor. They were published first by Leon Gautier in 1858 and in the later nineteenth century were subjected to critical analysis by Misset who regarded 45 sequences as authentic.[3] Blume, who edited the Victorine sequences in volumes 54 and 55 of the *Analecta Hymnica,* attributed 48 to Adam's authorship.

Adam's poetical concepts are centered in the mystical interpretation of biblical narratives and of Christian theology as it was taught in the schools of Paris. Hugh and Richard of St. Victor were his contemporaries but Adam was poet as well as theologian. Praise was to him an essential harmony of voice and life. His verse departed from the earlier prose rhythms of the German poets and was cast in a metrical form already popularized in the hymn. A group of rhymed trochaic lines of eight syllables with a caesura after the fourth syllable at the the end of a word, closes with a seven syllable line. This scheme with its many variants characterizes the work of Adam and his imitators in countless Latin and later, vernacular lyrics. Adam's sequence for the Feast of St. Stephen has been selected as illustrative of his finest work.
(See Illustrative Hymns, XIII. *Heri mundus exultavit,* "Yesterday with exultation.")

To appreciate fully the function of the sequence in worship at this time as well as its appeal to popular imagination, one should isolate a single theme for more intimate enjoyment. For this purpose, the sequences written for the five feasts of the Virgin are best suited. While manifold saints were honored in the hymnology of the day, the veneration of the Virgin reached at this time, its pinnacle of expression. Notker had provided sequences for her Nativity, Purification and Assumption. Adam of St. Victor, poet of the Virgin, drew upon all the resources of medieval symbolism in his *Salve, redemptoris mater,* "Hail, mother of the Redeemer," a masterpiece of medieval religious verse. Clerical poets everywhere met the challenge of his example. The result was indicative not only of their devotion and their poetic skill which was at times indifferent, but of the actual use of the Virgin sequences in the numerous feasts which honored her and their familiarity to wide congregations of clergy and laity.

During this period great sequence writers appeared, some known and distinguished, the majority anonymous. To the latter group belongs the author of the Easter sequence, *Victimae paschali laudes,* "Christians, to the

Paschal Victim," which represents the transition between the Notkerian and Victorine styles. The growing relationship between Latin hymnology and the arts becomes obvious in this sequence which was of importance in building the liturgical drama for Easter. The dialogue embedded in the poem,

"Speak, Mary, declaring
What thou sawest wayfaring?"

and her reply, ending

"Yea, Christ my hope is arisen:
To Galilee he goes before you."

contributed, with other sources, to the fully developed Easter Play.

The so-called Golden Sequence for Pentecost, *Veni sancte spiritus,* "Come, thou Holy Spirit, come,"[4] also of undetermined authorship, attained perhaps the greatest prestige, having now been heard in Christian worship for more than eight hundred years.

The activities of the French school are largely responsible for the popularity of sequences in the twelfth century and for their multiplication in every part of western Europe. Other factors played a part. Just as the Latin hymn can best be understood in the historical setting of the late Roman Empire or of the early Germanic kingdoms, so the development of the sequence must be interpreted in connection with the social and cultural environment of the age. The universities, notably that of Paris, were dominating intellectual life. Economic opportunity offered by the revival and expansion of craftsmanship, commerce, urban life and geographical knowledge resembled the achievement of Roman days. The European centralized states had emerged and were assuming the national features which mark them today. The modern languages of Europe were highly developed in their literary treasures and in everyday speech. Under reforming popes such as Innocent III, the church was entering an era of unity and spiritual renewal. Side by side with the reformed Benedictine Order, the Augustinian canons with their ancient prestige, the Franciscan, Dominican and other religious orders were taking their part in the work for the regeneration of society and the triumph of the Faith. Pilgrimages and crusades were in vogue for two hundred years from 1095. The hymnody of the church took on new vitality in an era of European awakening.

II. Later Hymns

Although the sequence had apparently occupied the center of attention, the writing of office and festival hymns had never been interrupted and certainly had never ceased. Gathering up the sources after the period of ninth century influence described in Chapter Three, one pauses at the verse of Peter Damian, (988-1072), Cardinal Bishop of Ostia and Superior of the monks of the Holy Cross. His theme was the joys of paradise in the hymn *Ad perennis vitae fontem,* "To the fount of life eternal," a topic about which a distinguished hymnody was ultimately created.
(See Illustrative Hymns, XIV. *Ad perennis vitae fontem,* "To the fount of life eternal.")

Fulbert, Bishop of Chartres (d. 1028), is best known for his Easter hymn, *Chorus novae Ierusalem,* "The chorus of the New Jerusalem,"[5] in which the militant ideal in its knightly form finds expression as the warriors of the faith acclaim the victory of their royal and divine leader.

In the twelfth century, a complete new hymnary in all its parts was written by Abelard, (1079-1142), for the Convent of the Paraclete of which Heloise was the abbess.[6] A collection of 91 hymns, it has never been highly praised by critics, yet it has provided the hymn, *O quanta qualia,* "How mighty are the Sabbaths," in praise of the Sabbath and the Good Friday hymn, *Solus ad victimam procedis, Domine,* "Alone to sacrifice Thou goest, Lord," both of which have found a place in recent hymnals. Helen Waddell's translations of the two illustrate modern renderings at their best. The same century saw the achievement of Bernard of Cluny or Morlaix, (fl. 1122), whose long poem, *De contemptu mundi* furnished the selections on the heavenly country, *Hora novissima,* popularized by the translations of John Mason Neale. Perhaps the best-known of these, *Urbs Sion aurea,* "Jerusalem the Golden," in its English rendering has attained a vernacular status independently of its Latin original. The great anonymous hymn, *Jesu dulcis memoria,* "Jesu, the very thought of Thee," is also of the twelfth century. Its authorship has been variously ascribed but never certainly determined.

The thirteen century was marked by the rise of hymn writing in the new religious orders founded by St. Francis of Assisi and St. Dominic.

The Franciscan Bonaventura (1221-74), wrote *Recordare sanctae crucis*, "Be mindful of the Holy Cross," on the theme of the Cross. To read this hymn side by side with the *Vexilla regis prodeunt* of Fortunatus, is to apprehend more fully the increasing subjectivity of the Latin hymn in 500 years of its history. The passion of Christ is, moreover, a favorite theme and object of devotion of the friars, ever present to their thinking. Thomas Aquinas, (1227-74), greatest of the Dominicans, wrote the hymns for the Feast of Corpus Christi, established by Pope Urban IV in 1265. Of these, *Pange lingua, gloriosi corporis mysterium*, "Sing my tongue, the Saviour's glory,"[7] modeled after the form of the *Pange lingua* of Fortunatus, is in its subject matter a poetic version of the mystical subtleties implicit in the dogma of the feast. John Peckham, Archbishop of Canterbury, (1240-92), wrote *Ave vivens hostia*, "Hail, true Victim," a fine hymn upon the same theme which suggests the inspiration of Aquinas.

III. Later Sequences

From the sequences of the later Middle Ages only a few have gained eminence but in certain cases as high a place as any in the whole range of their composition. Thomas Aquinas shows himself master of the sequence as well as the hymn in his *Lauda Sion Salvatorem*, "Praise, O Sion, praise thy Saviour," a model of the Victorine technique.
(See Illustrative Hymns, XV. *Lauda Sion Salvatorem*, 'Praise, O Sion, praise thy Saviour.")

Dies irae, "Day of wrath," most majestic of all sequences, universally acknowledged as the greatest achievement of Latin hymnology, was probably written by the Franciscan Thomas of Celano. It was originally used at Advent, later for All Souls' Day and for requiem masses. The Judgment theme is obviously inspired by the words of the Prophet Zephaniah (1: 15) from which the opening line *Dies irae, dies illa* is taken. A special literature, together with a multitude of translations, has grown up around this hymn which deserves consideration impossible here. It should be read not only with reference to its biblical sources but with the great Judgment portals of the medieval cathedrals in mind, since the sculpture and literature of the age here find a meeting place.[8] No less significant for its interpretation is the prevalence of the Black Death in the ages which produced it.[9] The thought of a period in which pain and death were so tragically familiar and before which the medieval man stood helpless, is faithfully reflected in contemporary hymns.

The lament in its poetic form is associated with the Marian hymnology of the fourteenth century. The *Stabat mater dolorosa*, "By the Cross her vigil keeping,"[10] its finest expression, like the *Dies irae*, needs little comment in these pages.
(See Illustrative Hymns, XVI. *Stabat mater dolorosa*, "By the Cross her vigil keeping.")

In this period it seems, at least to the present writer, that the Italian-born poets of the religious lyric come into their rightful heritage. The poets of England and of the French, German and Spanish-speaking lands had at one time or another held the palm in the field of hymnody. At the very moment, so to speak, when the genius of Dante and Petrarch had established the fame of Italian letters, the Christian hymn found new spokesmen in a literary medium which had originated in the same environment a thousand years before.

What has already been said of the multiplication of new feasts as the medieval ages progressed, is true in an even greater degree in the later centuries. The Feast of Corpus Christi is only one of many which marked this period of religious devotion, and incidentally required new sequences. If the collection of liturgical proses edited by Daniel in his *Thesaurus Hymnologicus* and reprinted in volumes 54 and 55 of the *Analecta Hymnica* be accepted as a guide, the new demands become clear. From the period of Adam of St. Victor, 174 feasts were furnished with sequences, many times over in the case of the more important festivals. The actual liturgical collections from which the *Analecta Hymnica* was compiled constitute a more specific source of information. If the attention of the student is fixed upon the sequences used in well-known missals and troparies from the thirteenth century and later, in the leading ecclesiastical centers of Europe, a wealth of material is revealed. Many of these sequences in the great collections are unfamiliar to the modern student, some have never been translated into English, but as a whole they are truly representative of this body of poetry in the period of its greatest interest. A tropary of St. Martial of the thirteenth century contains an anonymous Easter sequence, *Morte Christi celebrata* (*A. H.* 8. 33), "Christ's passion now is o'er,"[11] which bears comparison with the better-known sequences which have been named above.

IV. Liturgical Collections

To determine the actual usage of the hymn or sequence rather than its mere existence as a specimen of religious verse, the liturgical collection is indispensable. The old hymnaries and psalters and other books used in the offices were examined by liturgists of the period who compiled the breviaries of the later Middle Ages. Working under episcopal or monastic authority they subjected the hymnic material at their disposal to a selective process which necessarily discarded many hymns in favor of those rendered sacred by their inclusion in the old cycles, or of hymns of recognized merit. The Mozarabic Breviary had been compiled and its hymns determined by this process in an earlier century. After the re-conquest of the Spanish peninsula and the introduction of the Roman Rite in 1089, a version of the Roman Breviary was introduced. Episcopal centers in England, such as Hereford, York and primarily Salisbury, compiled their service books and developed them continuously to the close of the Middle Ages. The process was repeated throughout Christian Europe.

From the troparies and local collections of sequences the selections for the gradual and missal were made, just as the hymns had been for the breviary. These liturgical sources offer to the modern student the range of medieval hymnody at its best. The episcopal rites are, perhaps, more official and authoritative in their selection of hymns and sequences but the monastic rites often reveal the legends of local saints or the more intimate flavor of traditional piety. It should be understood that in countries where the Roman Rite prevailed there was no departure from its authority in the matter of hymnody. At the same time the greatest latitude was observable. A fine illustration is provided by the books of the Rite of Salisbury, England, or the Sarum Rite, which were compiled and developed by great liturgists from the time of Bishop Osmund in the eleventh century to the close of the Middle Ages. The Sarum Breviary contains 119 hymns, 25 of which were written after 1100 and the Missal contains 101 sequences, 54 of which were written about 1100.[12] The figures are revealing in the case of hymns, of the influence of the older cycles and in the case of sequences, of the multiplication of feasts in the later centuries of the Middle Ages.

The Processional book as a bearer of hymns will be treated in the following chapter. It remains here, to mention the Books of Hours or medieval Primers which also contained their quota of hymns. The *Horae* may be defined as a series of devotions, at first additional to the Seven Hours of the daily office but in the twelfth century elaborated in a separate book. Specifically the additions consisted of the penitential psalms, the Office of the Dead, the Cursus of All Saints, that of the Holy Cross, and that of the Blessed Virgin. Even before its separation from the Canonical Hours, the Cursus of the Blessed Virgin had assumed an importance which gave to the new collection its characteristic title of *Horae* or *Hours of the Blessed Virgin Mary.* In the fourteenth century the single volume came to be known in England as *Primarius Liber* or *Primarium* from which the more familiar name Prymer or Primer is derived.[13] Its popularity may be judged by the fact that 265 printed editions were later known in England and 1582 on the continent.[14] Hymns are interspersed throughout the *Horae.* In the York Hours there are eighteen hymns and sequences of varied periods of which thirteen are centered in devotion to the Virgin.[15] In other words, the hymns which were chosen for these books of popular devotion are representative of later medieval favorites in hymnody, indicating to what extent the older hymns were known and loved and to what extent later poems had been accepted by lay folk as well as clergy. The *Horae* are primarily valuable as a source for the later Marian hymns upon the themes of the Joys and of the Sorrows of the Virgin. The appearance of the beloved *Stabat mater dolorosa,* without doubt the finest expression of the poetry of sorrow, bears witness to the discriminative process by which the *Horae* were compiled. It seems remarkable that the liturgists of the later period, in which the Latin hymn was beginning to show signs of deterioration, were able to skirt as successfully as they did, the limits of trashy sentimentality and worse poetry which were passing current under the name of hymnody.

To those who are interested in the relations between literature and the fine arts an examination of the Virgin hymns, as of the *Dies Irae*, will yield similar interrelations. The hymns which were written from the twelfth century onwards upon the Virgin theme may be closely correlated with the sculptured forms which portray the Mother apart from the Son in her Sorrows and more particularly in her Joys, laden with her distinctive honors and regnant as the Queen of Heaven.

V. Influences affecting Hymnody

Once the typical hymns and sequences of the later period have been reviewed, it remains to trace the influences operating from the contemporary environment upon their evolution. The problem of possible influence of an ultimately oriental origin has already arisen in connection with earlier hymns. It has been considered in the relation of Byzantine culture to the origin of the sequence, and also in the form of Arabian influence upon the Mozarabic hymnody. In both fields the evidence is tenuous and especially in the latter where the imprint of Arabian cultural forms would seem to be most probable. In the centuries which produced the troubadours, the problem takes the form of a possible indirect influence from Arabian origins through the Provençal singers upon the evolution of the sequence.[16] It is true that the twelfth and thirteenth centuries boasted at least four hundred troubadours whose poetry is extant. The names of others are known but not their poems. As the popularity of their songs is unquestioned, an appreciable affect upon religious lyrics might be presumed. Granted that the influence of Arabian poetry may be demonstrated upon the metrical aspects of troubadour lyrics, it must still be demonstrated that the impact of the latter was felt upon the Latin hymn. Future studies may throw light upon these problems of medieval literature where obscurity now prevails. Metrical similarities undoubtedly exist between Arabian and Latin verse, as already illustrated in the field of late Mozarabic hymns. Perhaps the most convincing evidence, aside from these, is found in processional hymns, the subject of a later chapter.

Much more obvious and one distinctly to be traced is the all- pervading influence of the new religious orders upon medieval society and culture in general. Hymn writers belonging, as cited above, to the Franciscan, Dominican and other orders of friars, to say nothing of the Cistercians, played a leading role among contemporary poets; their names and themes have already been mentioned. Many others must be numbered with the anonymous majority. The veneration of the Virgin reflected so faithfully in contemporary hymns may be largely attributed to their devotion. As itinerant preachers, moreover, the friars translated hymns into the vernacular and brought them directly to their hearers, thus imparting the lessons of faith and morals.[17] It might be asserted, at least tentatively, that the friars were responsible for one of the earliest attempts to bridge the gap between the ritual and the popular use of hymns.

A less tangible influence was at work emanating from schoolmen. This was the age of the universities in which thousands of students were pursuing the studies of theology, law and medicine. Early theological discussion in the schools of Paris, prior to the founding of the universities, is implicit in the sequences of Adam of St. Victor. Later, Thomas Aquinas, Professor of Theology at the University of Paris, created a poetical counterpart in his hymns, to the prose exposition of dogma. No one else reached his stature in this particular but hundreds of European clerics having theological degrees or a partial preparation for them, were active in the church and in secular life. It is only fair to suppose that they must be included in the great anonymous group which assisted in making that unique contribution to medieval literature which was preserved in contemporary liturgical collections. Without the university-trained cleric how is it explicable that in the very age in which the vernacular languages came to their full development in speech and in literature, Latin religious verse was at a peak of expression? In the High Middle Ages the alumni of the great universities were influential in every phase of society. It is conceivable, if not demonstrable, that the clerics among their ranks played an important although hitherto unrecognized role in the evolution of Latin hymnody.

Contemporary pilgrimages take the student far afield from the centers of learning. The crusading enterprise of two centuries which carried the knightly companies of Europe and their entourage to the East was a pilgrimage of continental proportions. Local shrines favored by pilgrims abounded in the West from Canterbury and Walsingham to Campostella. What effect, if any, had this wave of religious zeal or of adventurous self-seeking upon the hymnology of the age? We know that the familiar Latin hymns of the breviary were sung by the clerics who conducted the services of religion in the crusading armies. We possess the texts of a variety of vernacular hymns and songs heard among the wandering bands who traversed the highways of Europe or traveled by sea to distant shrines. We are told of the singing of Latin hymns at the destination of pilgrimage but their texts are rare. A formal collection of Latin hymns associated with the shrine of St. James of Campostella, the *Carmina Campostellana*, has been edited in the seventeenth volume of the *Analecta Hymnica*. As might be supposed, they voice the praises of St. James, *Ad honorem regis summi*, "To the honor of the King," (*A. H.* 17. 210) being a favorite in both Latin and vernacular versions.[18] As a matter of fact, the hymnody of pilgrimage must have been largely patronal, a conclusion supported by existing Latin texts. Unfortunately we possess no great body of Latin hymns arising from the religious impulse which animated the crusader or the devotee of local shrines. It is possible, however, that the multiplication of hymns for saints at this time may be attributed in part to the multiplication of shrines of pilgrimage. If true, an influence is seen at work, which, from the time when Ambrose built a church in Milan to receive the relics of St. Gervasius and St. Protasius and wrote a hymn in their honor, never ceased to operate in the intervening centuries.[19]

With the pilgrim we come face to face with the layman and are once more confronted with the question of lay participation in the singing of Latin hymns, which hinges upon the further question of the degree to which the layman could sing or even understand the Latin hymn, from the twelfth century onward. The pious injunctions of Alexander of Hales and Henricus de Gorichen (15th C.) to sing hymns, merely repeat a dictum of St. Apollonius regarding the observance of the Lord's Day in the second century and must not be taken too seriously by the modern student.[20] It is indeed slight evidence for the singing of Latin hymns by the laity. The problem is in reality linguistic and revolves about the question of who was acquainted with Latin at this time. Setting aside the clergy in their numerous ranks, who are often said to have had the complete monopoly of the hymn in an age when congregational singing was unknown, one must consider the remaining classes of society from the point of view of contemporary education.

Beginning with the university it should be recalled that the text books and other sources of information were in Latin and that Latin was the medium of instruction. In this respect the aspirant for a degree in law or medicine was on a par with the would-be clergyman. Many students took degrees in two and occasionally in all three disciplines, and the majority were destined for the church if only in minor orders. On the other hand, it is certain that, as in our own day, a large number of students never attained any degree although they had the Latin qualification. In any case, the lay alumnus or former student of the universities, with a Latin training, was a familiar figure in secular affairs.

The degree and extent of elementary and secondary education upon which the university instruction was necessarily founded, have been the subject of several recent studies. It seems certain that schools for children and youth existed from the ninth century onward in cathedral and other centers and that, as Lynn Thorndike says, "in the period of developed medieval culture elementary education was fairly wide-spread and general."[21] Without entering into the details of this program, illuminating as they are, we note that the curriculum was founded upon the Latin language and Latin studies. The contemporary growth of towns involved an expansion of education which was marked by the appearance of schools sponsored by municipal authority. The Latin school flourished everywhere. There is evidence that every social class participated to some extent in the new education although illiteracy must at the same time have been common. It seems clear that the layman who had received these early educational advantages could understand Latin hymns or read them if the texts were available. Both sexes shared elementary education and lay women as well as nuns occasionally had access to advanced instruction. Such considerations as the above presuppose a degree of familiarity especially with the breviary hymns, on the part of laymen, even if singing or chanting was restricted to the choirs and clergy.

The university movement was accompanied by the rise of the wandering scholars and poets whose verses, for example, from the *Carmina*

Burana, are familiar today in translation. Popular entertainers, they sang their Latin lyrics at ale house doors and in the market places. They must have been at least partially understood by the populace. Other municipal entertainment was provided by the religious drama of the times which made considerable demand upon the Latin resources of the spectator who had to be somewhat bilingual if he were to enjoy the public presentation of the mystery plays.

Again, the bilingual or macaronic poetry which sprang up in the period of rivalry between Latin and the vernacular may be viewed both as a means and a result of understanding Latin hymns. Macaronic verse was both secular and religious in its forms, favorite phrases from well-known Latin hymns often being combined with the vernacular tongue. The practice might even have spread to the ritual of the Church had it not been forbidden by ecclesiastical decree.[22] The *cantio* of the later medieval centuries and the familiar carol offer a wealth of evidence that macaronic religious verse was extremely popular. Indeed, this may have been the earliest manifestation of actual hymn singing on the part of medieval laymen.

Even if congregational singing was not practiced, the use of Latin hymns in private devotion is well authenticated. The *Horae* which were included in the liturgical collections listed above, were circulated among laymen from the fourteenth century onward, and often used as text books or Primers from which children were taught to read. The variant title, *Lay Folks Prayer Book,* also bespeaks its popular availability.

While it would be unsound to infer a universal knowledge of Latin hymnody among the laity of Europe upon any or all of the evidence here assembled, it is logical to suppose that this treasury of verse lay within the boundaries of average education and cultural ability. Combined with the effectiveness of visual means of conveying religious truths through architecture, sculpture and stained glass, popular acquaintance with the teachings of Christian hymnody must be supposed to have overflowed the limits of clerical restriction, if indeed, any such existed.

VI. Characteristics

To close this somewhat rambling account of the Latin hymn and sequence in the later medieval centuries, which is necessarily discursive even as the civilization itself was everywhere expanding, the characteristics of this poetry should be reviewed in comparison with those of earlier Latin hymns.

An increasing variety of subject matter is first to be noted, to accompany the diversification of worship brought about by new feasts and the appearance of new religious agencies. Hymns for the festivals of saints provide the best illustrations of this tendency which has been amply treated above.

A marked trend toward the compilation of local liturgical collections and the differentiation of service books accompanies the unification of rites in various European lands. This tendency was observed in earlier centuries, particularly in Spain where the Mozarabic hymnal prevailed. St. Gall had provided a monastic center of influence in German-speaking lands in its day. Now, the great diocesan and monastic centers, on a much larger scale, are furnished with a full complement of ritual books and guides to hymnody. In England, the Sarum collection achieved great prominence, acquiring national rather than diocesan proportions.

Within the hymnic poetry itself changes are seen both in form and spirit. A full development of metrical forms takes place, some of which had appeared much earlier in isolated examples and were now widely accepted; others were characteristic of late medieval literary art. The meters and rhythm of sequence poetry were popularly favored. Subjective qualities and attitudes which had been infrequent in the earlier hymns devoted to biblical themes and theological expression are much more obvious in later hymns. The personal petition and the direct address to deity and the saints are frequent. It has been suggested above in considering hymns upon the theme of the Cross, that a comparison of hymns from the earlier and later groups is instructive. But any of the great themes may be selected for this purpose, for example, the Pentecostal theme, with a group of hymns in which the earlier ones are simple narratives following the biblical account of the descent of the Holy Spirit; the later ones are exemplified by *Veni, sancte spiritus*, "Come, Thou Holy Spirit, come," already cited, in which the Spirit is addressed and invoked for personal blessings and the sevenfold gifts.

With the waning of the medieval centuries came a characteristic decadence in the poetical quality of Latin hymns and in their spiritual vitality. This was true of the sequence and most obvious, perhaps, in those which were devoted to the praise of the saints. Reference to this phenomenon will be made in a later chapter in connection with the possible reason for the loss of religious significance which must be admitted although deplored by students of the subject.

Finally, one observes that certain hymns of these later centuries rival, if not surpass, the representative hymns of the first half of the Middle Ages. Four of the five sequences retained in the present-day Roman Missal were all selected from this group, namely: *Lauda Sion Salvatorem, Veni sancte spiritus, Dies Irae,* and *Stabat mater dolorosa.* Other illustrative hymns and sequences mentioned above prove to be almost as familiar.

On the contrary, decadent hymns have tended to disappear. Unworthy of their theme and purpose, a multitude of examples may be unearthed from their present burial places in the *Analecta Hymnica* or other collections by the curious investigator. So far as actual usage is concerned they have been gradually discarded and forgotten in the process of time. Similarly those of greater merit have possessed a survival value sufficient to insure recognition in every succeeding century.

CHAPTER SIX

Late Middle Ages: Processional Hymns

I. Origins

The procession as a practice of the Christian Church originates in the triumphal entry of Jesus into Jerusalem. All four evangelists record the event and all four make mention of the hosannas and acclamations of the people which accompanied it.[1] True, the procession is older than Christianity and wider in observance. It seems to be a natural impulse of humanity in all ages and in all lands to make orderly progress from one place to another for the expression of communal joy or lamentation or to seek the aid and blessing of supernatural power in the activities and vicissitudes of life.

Processional ceremonies as they were observed in ancient oriental civilizations or in the culture of Greece and Rome are not considered here, except as they may have affected Christian origins. The purpose of this chapter is to describe the background and setting of processional forms which, in their evolution, gave rise to a continuity of hymns; to trace the origin, development and distinguishing features of such processional hymns in the Middle Ages and to display processional hymnody in its distinctive character as a separate category of medieval Latin hymnology.

Prior to the fourth century the record is obscure. Miscellaneous notices begin to appear in the last quarter of the century. Basil notes a procession in the form of a litany (c. 375). Ambrose mentions a procession of monks (c. 388) and also refers to a procession in Rome honoring Sts. Peter and Paul, in his hymn, *Apostolorum passio*, "The passion of the Apostles," (*A. H.* 50. 17): Chrysostom was active in organizing processions in Constantinople to offset Arian influence (390-400).[2] At the same period, 379-388, Aetheria (St. Sylvia of Aquitania?) made her pilgrimage to the holy places of Palestine, describing in her journal in detail, the ceremonies enacted in the worship of the Christian Church at Jerusalem.[3]

Remarkable in all respects, Aetheria's narrative is obviously written in a spirit of devotion with eager curiosity and joyful appreciation. She describes, among other observances, the Hour services, especially the *lucernare* when hymns were sung, the Sunday procession to the Anastasis or Church of the Resurrection which marked the tomb of Jesus and the procession and rites for the Feasts of the Epiphany, Ypapanti or Presentation of Christ in the temple, Palm Sunday and Easter.[4] Hymns in which the laity as well as the clergy participated are mentioned in connection with these ceremonies but no specific hymn is named. The immediate purpose of the processions at Jerusalem appears to have been the enactment of scenes in the life of Jesus in the places where they occurred, introducing a dramatic element which pervades medieval processional observances throughout their history.

Aetheria uses the words psalm, antiphon and hymn in connection with the musical parts of the worship she observed, but not indiscriminately. She was probably familiar with hymns as they had developed in the fourth century both in the eastern and western churches. It has been assumed that the hymn sung at the daily lighting of the candles was *Phos hilaron*, "O gladsome light."[5] The hymns she heard at the Good Friday observance have been tentatively identified as the *Idiomela* for Good Friday, traditional in Byzantine ritual.[6] In any case they were true hymns, perhaps of a metrical, or more probably of a rhythmical type. It is impossible to identify the processional hymns of which she speaks. All that can be asserted is that non-scriptural, as well as scriptural hymns, were sung in the processions at Jerusalem.

In Constantinople, contemporary processions have already been mentioned. The practice of Jerusalem was also adopted there. In the sixth century under Justinian, the Feast of Ypapanti was introduced.[7] However, the history of Byzantine processions must be omitted from this study which is devoted primarily to the Latin West.

In Rome, the Christian procession had an independent origin, being derived in part from the memorial honors paid to the Christian martyrs and in part from the Christianization of pagan ceremonies. When the period of persecution of Christianity had come to a close and the triumphant Church was able to assert publicly her influence and authority at Rome, processions were made as early as the fifth century to the places where martyrs had suffered. This is the origin of the later station procession, followed by the celebration of mass in the various churches where the remains of martyrs removed from the catacombs were buried. A century earlier in Milan, Ambrose had discovered and removed the bodies of St. Protasius and of St. Gervasius from their original burial place to a church newly erected in their honor.[8] Pope Gregory the Great (590-604) observed the Roman stations and Pope Sergius (687-701) completed their organization.[9] The processions were accompanied by the chanting of psalms but there is no record of non-scriptural hymns. The symbolism of the procession, however, was enriched by the idea of pilgrimage to a spot made sacred by martyrdom, a continuing processional motive throughout the Middle Ages.

While the station processions developed in the vicinity of Rome, the litany processions arose in Gaul. Mametus, the Bishop of Vienne, 474, inaugurated the *litania minor* or the public blessing of the fields and crops in the spring season. In 511, the Council of Orleans ordained the observance for Gaul, and the Council of Girona, in 517, for Spain. The *litaniae minores* or rogations, perpetuate in their intent, processions of the Roman era. The *litaniae maiores* which were prescribed by Gregory the Great, 598, and Leo III (795-816), were of similar origin and purpose. A *litania septiformis* was also organized by Gregory on the occasion of a pestilence at Rome.[10] The *litania maior* came to be observed on April 25, St. Mark's day, and the *litaniae minores* in the three days preceding Ascension. Psalms but not hymns in the sense of non-scriptural compositions were heard in the litanies. The procession of supplication common alike to pagan and Christian practice is illustrated in the litanies, a constant motive and a constant observance in medieval rites.

It seems clear, therefore, that primitive Christian processions in Rome consisted of stations and litanies. Festival processions were introduced into the west gradually. Ascension is spoken of as an ancient feast but there is no specific evidence of its observance before the middle of the fourth century. The Ascension procession, implied by Aetheria in her journal, is unknown in Rome at this time.[11] Pope Sergius imported into Rome the festival procession for Candlemas or the Feast of the Purification of the Virgin. The Feast of Ypapanti or Presentation, originally observed in Jerusalem and later adopted in Constantinople, as noted above, gained in the transfer a new feature. The carrying of lighted candles, not mentioned by Aetheria, seems to have been added in Byzantine practice. The words spoken by Simeon of the infant Jesus, "a light to lighten the Gentiles" (Luke 2. 32) made the symbolic use of lights almost inevitable. The date of the Feast of the Purification, February 2, was approximately that of the pagan *Amburbium* or *Amburbale,* an early Roman procession of lustration which had taken place in that month. Possibly the procession for the Feast is reminiscent of this pagan practice.[12] It might be of interest to follow in closer detail the origin of the medieval Candlemas, but attention must be directed to the Candlemas hymns later to be written and sung in procession at this Feast.

The period of Christian processional origins which may be considered to close with the seventh century, saw the development of the processions at Jerusalem, their adoption in Constantinople and the evolution of the stations and litanies in the west. Festival processions also, were slowly making their way into the Western Church.[13]

II. Evolution in the Early Middle Ages

That the Latin processional hymn appeared first in Gaul should surprise no one. It has already been suggested that the hymns among the *Carmina* of Fortunatus were created in the atmosphere of freedom enjoyed by Gallic hymn writers in accordance with contemporary canons. Always a poet of the occasion, Fortunatus wrote three hymns for the reception of a relic believed to be of the true Cross, which was presented to Rhadegunda, his patron, by the Byzantine Emperor, Justin II and his wife Sophia, for the convent at Poitiers. As a final stage in the journey from Constantinople, the relic was borne in procession from Migné to Poitiers, accompanied by Euphronius, Bishop of Tours. On this day the hymn, *Vexilla regis prodeunt,* was first heard.[14] Two others, *Pange lingua* and *Crux benedicta* (see Chapter One) were devoted by Fortunatus to the same theme of the Holy Cross, although it cannot be proved that they were sung in the same procession.

The Resurrection hymn, *Tempora florigero rutilant distincta sereno,* "Season of luminous days, marked bright with the birth of flowers," (*Carm.* 3. 9), was originally written for the Easter baptismal rites celebrated by Felix, Bishop of Nantes (d. 582). It was a poem of 110 lines or 55 elegiac couplets, from which the cento of 28 lines beginning *Salve festa dies,* "Hail thee, festival day," was later selected for an Easter processional.[15]

The metrical models provided by *Pange lingua* of the trochiac pattern and *Salve festa dies,* the elegiac, continued to be employed throughout the Middle Ages for processional hymnody, the elegiac excelling in popularity. First in the original hymn, then in centos and finally in imitative verse adapted to a multitude of feasts, *Salve festa dies* was never superseded but maintained the influence of Fortunatus for centuries.

Spain must have known the processional hymn soon after its appearance in Gaul, perhaps in the seventh century. Here, the Palm Sunday festival seems to have been the source of inspiration for the procession and blessing of palms is mentioned by Isidore of Seville as an observance of his day.[16] Contemporary evidence indicates a similar procession in Italy.[17] The use of a processional hymn, however, is not as clearly indicated.

It seems probable that the seventh century hymn, *Magnum salutis gaudium* (*A.H.* 51. 73), "O great joy of salvation," is one of the earliest to be assigned for Palm Sunday. It is a simple rendering in the Ambrosian style, of the events recounted in the biblical narrative.[18] In the early centuries when the concept of a specific processional hymn for a particular festival was almost unheard of, a familiar hymn from the old hymnals might be used in the new ceremonies. It has been suggested that *Magnum salutis gaudium* was known to Theodulphus, who in the ninth century wrote the Palm Sunday processional hymn, *Gloria laus et honor,* for all the ages.

Processions, thus far, have been thought of chiefly, as wholly or in part outside the church edifice. Processions within the edifice were also frequently observed. A procession of the clergy, in connection with which psalms and antiphons were sung, preceded the Sunday high mass; another took place as the Gospel codex was carried to its place for reading. Other ceremonies within the church, aside from the liturgy proper, were sometimes accompanied by hymns.[19]

Perhaps the earliest hymn in use at a special ceremony, once more a selection from the hymnal, was *Audi, iudex mortuorum* (*A. H.* 51. 80), "Hear Thou Judge of the dead," sung on Holy Thursday at the consecration of the chrism.[20] The words *O redemptor, sume carmen temet concinentium,* "O Redeemer, accept the hymn of Thy people magnifying Thee,"[21] formed a refrain, a metrical feature which came to be the unmistakable mark of the processional hymn.

In this early period from the sixth to the tenth century, a new idea and a new practice came into being, the use of hymns apart from those of the canonical hours and the sequences of the mass. The ninth century revival of hymnody in all its branches was taking place in western Europe just as this period came to a close, in connection with which the processional hymn was inevitably affected as the office hymn and the sequence had been by a fresh inspiration to poetry and worship. The movement came to fruition at St. Gall where the musical and ceremonial aspects of that great monastic center were so highly developed, a center which had contributed so heavily to the Carolingian revival of literature and the arts.

The French liturgical scholar, Leon Gautier, whose contributions to the study of medieval hymnology have already been mentioned, was the first to identify the processional hymn as a trope or liturgical interpolation. In a study of the St. Gall processional hymns he observed that they were classified by the name *versus* which in itself points to a separate hymnic category. Other earlier hymns used in processions were there called *versus.* Gautier discovered that musical notation always appeared with the *versus,* an indication that these hymns were invariably chanted and he noted that the *versus,* in the manner of the hymn *O redemptor, sume carmen,* cited above, was without exception, accompanied by a refrain.[22]

The processional hymns of St. Gall, like the sequences, bore the characteristic marks of the hymnic group to which they belonged. From this stage in their evolution they were set apart by their music, classification and refrain.

The wider circle of Carolingian liturgical interest included hymn writers other than those of St. Gall: Theodulphus of Orleans, Walafrid Strabo of Richenau, Rabanus Maurus of Fulda, Radbert of Corbie, who with Waldram and Hartmann of St. Gall wrote processional hymns. The hymns of Theodulphus and of Rabanus Maurus have been considered above.

Other great festivals of the ecclesiastical year and of the saints were now observed with processional honors for which new hymns were written; special ceremonies also, were thus recognized. Hartmann wrote the elegiac hymn *Salve, lacteolo decoratum sanguine festum* (*A. H.* 50. 251), "Hail festival, graced with the blood of the Innocents," for the Feast of the Holy Innocents. The processional hymns of Rabanus Maurus were heard at Nativity, Easter and possibly the Feast of the Purification. The dramatic spirit, always present in the true processional is felt in all these hymns while the refrain reiterates the message of the feast:
for Easter,

R. Surrexit quia Christus a sepulcro,
Collaetetur homo choro angelorum. (*A.H.* 50. 190)

Since Christ has risen from the tomb,
Let man rejoice with the choir of angels.

for the Nativity,

R. Christo nato, rege magno
totuş orbis gaudeat. (*A. H.* 50. 186)

Since Christ is born, the mighty king,
let the whole earth rejoice.

Processional hymns for saints are represented by Radbert's hymn honoring St. Gall,

R. Annua, sancte Dei, celebramus festa diei,
Qua, pater, e terris sidera, Galle, petis. (*A. H.* 50. 241)

We celebrate, O Saint of God, our yearly feast on this day
When thou, father Gallus, dost leave the earth for heaven.

To celebrate the life and miracles of a patron saint was frequently the inspiration of a medieval procession, which, in the case of St. Gall, passed beyond the precincts of the monastery into the streets of the town.[23] It is no wonder that the tradition of these processions, furnished with all the splendor of festival vestments, of robed choirs, of monastic treasures and sacred banners should have made St. Gall unique.

The Sunday processions were sometimes accompanied by imposing hymns in the form of litanies. It should not be forgotten that the ancient Christian processions were, in great part, of this nature. Waldram, Hartmann and Radbert wrote such hymns but Hartmann's was evidently a favorite, *Summus et omnipotens genitor, qui cuncta creasti,* "Mighty and omnipotent father, who hast created all things," with the refrain,

R. Humili prece et sincera devotione
Ad te clamantes semper exaudi nos. (*A. H.* 50. 253)

With humble prayer and pure devotion,
Ever hear us as we cry to Thee.

It seems probable that the custom of singing a hymn in the procession before the reading of the Gospel originated at St. Gall. Hartmann provided a beautiful *versus* for this purpose,

Sacrata libri dogmata
Portantur evangelici. (*A. H.* 50. 250)

The sacred words of the
Gospel are borne.

A *versus* for the reception of the Eucharist was written by Radbert, *Laudes omnipotens, ferimus tibi dona colentes* (*A. H.* 50. 239), "In reverence, Almighty, we bring our praises as gifts to Thee." The Blessing of the Font on Holy Saturday inspired his *Versus ad Descensum fontis* (*A. H.* 50. 242-3). Among the ceremonies most characteristic of medieval piety was that of *Mandatum* or foot-washing, commemorating the act of Jesus in washing his disciples' feet, (*John* 13; 1-15). The name "Maundy Thursday" is a modern survival of the ancient terminology.[24] The hymn associated with this rite appears first in Gaul in the eighth or ninth century and may have been current in Italy in monastic centers. The antiphon, *Ubi caritas et amor, Deus ibi est,* "Where charity is and love, God is there," is at once the motive and refrain of this hymn, *Congregavit nos in unum Christi amor* (*A.H.* 12. 24), "The love of Christ has united us," which follows the scriptural account.[25]

The student must turn once more to the great monastic centers of the Germanic world for processional hymns honoring royalty. Visits of kings and emperors to St. Gall and other noted monasteries were by no means uncommon; that colorful processions and demonstrations of loyalty were a part of their reception cannot be doubted. Walafrid Strabo celebrates the visit of Lothair to Reichenau with the hymn,

R. Imperator magne, vivas
semper et feliciter. (*A.H.* 50. 176)

Live, O mighty emperor
ever in felicity.

Walafrid Strabo praised Charles, son of Louis the Pious, and Radbert, the Empress Richgard. Other processionals could be used on the occasion of the coming of any royal visitor.

Vatican manuscripts offer evidence of contemporary processions in Italy and Rome, the city of their origin. From this source is derived the processional hymn *Sancta Maria, quid est?* (*A.H.* 23. 74), "Sancta Maria, what meaneth this?" written for the procession which marked the eve of the Feast of the Assumption, about the year 1000. Specific directions for the route, the order of precedence and every detail of the ceremonial are available, while the hymn itself depicts the devotion and human appeal attending this night time scene in Rome.[26]

III. Evolution in the Later Middle Ages

For the evolution of the processional hymn from this point to the close of the Middle Ages, we have in addition to hymnic manuscripts, the service books and manuals devoted to, or including, processional practice. The *Ritual* or *Roman Pontifical* was the earliest to include directions for processions, an illustration of which has been presented above in the case of *Sancta Maria, quid est?* In the course of time, since so many medieval processions were not thus provided for, the *Processional* came into existence, containing the order of processions for a particular diocese or monastery.[27] The St. Gall *Processionals,* for instance, are informative as to customs already described above. The specific name *versus* gave rise to the title *Versarius* for a book of processional hymns.[28]

In addition to the collections, liturgical writers discussed the procession. Of these, none was more influential than Durandus, Bishop of Mende, who, about 1286, produced his *Rationale divinorum officiorum* which among many other liturgical subjects, included processional rites.[29] Durandus was a leading authority upon ecclesiastical symbolism. Accordingly, he dwells upon every minute detail of the great processions for Easter, Ascension, Palm Sunday and the Purification as well as the Sunday procession and others of lesser importance, ascribing to each act a wealth of symbolic meaning. Much of this figurative interpretation is obvious and inherent in the feast to be celebrated but in other cases he gives full play to his sense of the symbolic, a phase of contemporary thought already so characteristic of Adam of St. Victor and other writers on religious themes. Finally he declares that whatever else is suggested, "the true procession is a progress to the celestial country." (*Ipse vero processio, est via ad coelestem patriam.*)[30] If the fundamental concepts which entered into their origins be reviewed, medieval processions apparently carried with them the familiar ideas of supplication, of dramatic representation or of pilgrimage to sacred places. Durandus reiterates and sublimates these concepts, giving them an added significance.

The processional manuals, especially of the English rites observed at Salisbury, York, Canterbury and other cathedral centers, offer descriptions and sometimes illustrations showing the order and vestments of the clergy, the position and functions of the choir, the appropriate acts involved, together with the complete text of the antiphons, psalms, other scriptural passages, hymns, prayers and rubrics. Turning to the processional hymns which were rendered in these centuries, one is impressed by the gradual disappearance of hymns typical of the efforts of the St. Gall school and its contemporaries. A tremendous vogue of the original *Salve festa dies* of Fortunatus which had never been lost sight of, together with its centos, variants and copies, takes possession of the field. There were in all, perhaps, from one hundred to one hundred and fifty true processional hymns in circulation throughout the whole medieval period, if one enumerates those which are edited in the *Analecta Hymnica.* One half of these may be considered to be of the *Salve festa dies* type while similar elegiac metrical forms are found in half of the remainder.

What has been said of the cultural background in which the sequence developed and multiplied is equally true for the processional hymn. The same influences which created new seasonal feasts and additional feasts for the saints, produced new processional hymns to accompany them. There is, however, a great disparity between the number of sequences and processional hymns that were written. The sequence was regnant in sacred and secular verse, both in Latin and the vernaculars. Office hymns, too, far outnumbered processionals. This may be another way of saying that the office hymns and the sequences had a liturgical function and setting, while the processional was always extra-liturgical and either superfluous or purely ornamental from this point of view. The antiphons and psalms were sufficient to satisfy the essential choral demands of any procession.

Unfortunately Thomas Aquinas did not include a processional hymn when he furnished the hymnody for the Feast of Corpus Christi. He could hardly have envisaged the thousands of Corpus Christi processions throughout Catholic Christendom which have marked the Feast even to this day. Nor could he have foreseen that his hymn *Pange lingua gloriosi corporis mysterium,* written in the tradition of Fortunatus, would be widely appropriated for that purpose. Other processionals for Corpus Christi appeared almost at once, especially of the *Salve* type.

Contemporary devotion to the Virgin Mother and her festivals was felt in the expansion of the Marian hymnology for processions. The establishment of St. Osyth in Essex was a center in which new hymns were used for the Visitation,

Salve festa dies, toto venerabilis aevo,
  Qua Christi mater visitat Elizabeth. (*A. H.* 11. 51)

Hail thee, festival day, blest day that is hallowed forever,
  On which Christ's mother visits Elizabeth.

and the Assumption,

Salve festa dies, toto venerabilis aevo,
Qua fuit assumpta virgo Maria pia. (*A.H.* 11. 55)

———

Hail thee, festival day, blest day that is hallowed forever,
On which the holy Virgin Mary was assumed.

A lengthy hymn of twenty stanzas for the Feast of the Purification which had been observed for so many centuries, appears in a twelfth or thirteenth century manuscript from Kremsmünster, *Laetetur omne saeculum* (*A. H.* 4. 54), "Let every age rejoice." The biblical scene of the Presentation in the Temple is described and reference is made to the carrying of lighted candles.

Later medieval practice perpetuated other earlier customs. From the original station processions at Rome had developed the ceremonies to celebrate the translation of relics of saints in western European lands. Pope Callistus II (d. 1124) wrote a processional hymn honoring St. James of Campostella, *Versus Calixti Papae, cantandi ad processionem sancti Jacobi in solemnitate passionis ipsius et translatione ejusdem* (*A. H.* 17. 194), or *Versus of Pope Callistus, to be sung at the procession of St. James in the celebration of his passion and translation.* A hymn for St. Kyneburga (d. 680) commemorated the restoration of her relics to their original burial place in Peterborough Minster from which they had been removed during the Danish invasions.[31] (*A. H.* 43. 218)

A procession in which the relics were carried for the veneration of the worshipers was familiar in many places. Records from St. Gall testify that St. Magnus was honored with such a procession and an appropriate hymn of praise (*A. H.* 50. 261). The relics of saints treasured at Exeter were borne in procession with the singing of a hymn which mentions their miraculous powers. (*A. H.* 43. 277)

In an era marked by municipal drama and civic display as well as religious festivals, the pageantry of the procession was understandably popular. Rome always had its great processions. Accounts are extant of ceremonies accompanied by hymns, in Tournai, Strasburg, Nuremberg and other medieval towns, aside from those prescribed by episcopal and monastic manuals of the day for the great cathedrals and abbeys.

The music to which the processional hymn was sung is, in some cases, available. The St. Gall manuscripts, as Gautier noted, were furnished with musical notation. This is occasionally true of later manuscripts, especially as we enter the closing medieval centuries. The traditional melodies of certain hymns, like the *Salve festa dies* and *Gloria laus et honor* are known to-day. Musicologists and students of liturgical music are currently engaged in bringing this music to present-day knowledge. For example, the hymn used in procession before the reading of the Gospel appears in the twelfth and thirteenth centuries as a *conductus* or *conductum* which, in turn, is related to the *cantio*.[32] A *conductus* for the festival of St. James of Campostella (*A. H.* 17. 199), illustrates the evolution of a minor type of processional hymn from Hartmann's solemn *versus*, mentioned above, to the festive style of the late medieval period. The recent study of the *conductus* by Leonard Ellinwood reflects the growing interest of musicians in these forms, both secular and religious, which preceded the Renaissance.[33]

To summarize the characteristic marks of the processional hymn which are constant and quite independent of the date of their appearance, the student must recall the underlying motives: 1) supplication in the litanies, 2) re-enactment of biblical scenes and 3) religious pilgrimage. Respecting usage, the special interest of a ceremony devoted to a particular occasion is present in processional hymns, additional to other rites. Lastly, a group of hymns has come into existence, not to be classified with the more formal categories of the office hymn and the sequence but dedicated to an extra-liturgical purpose.

As a group, the processional hymns are not well-known or frequently used in translation with the exception of the ageless hymns of Theodulphus and especially of Fortunatus whose processionals usurped the medieval field for over one thousand years and are still current to-day.

(See Illustrative Hymns, XVII. *Salve festa dies,* "Hail thee, festival day.")

CHAPTER SEVEN

Influence and Survival of Latin Hymns

I. Late Medieval Influence

From the creation of the Latin hymn in the fourth century by the earliest writers to the efforts of poets heralding the Renaissance, Christian hymnody left its imprint upon contemporary verse both secular and religious. The field of inquiry suggested by this thesis has never been fully explored although it abounds in fascinating possibilities for the student of medieval culture. The subject, of course, cannot be treated within the limits of this chapter but such hints may be offered as have resulted from a partial study of particular areas or fall within the bounds of reasonable assumption.

Perhaps the most pervading influence and the simplest to trace is the metrical. The iambic dimeter of Ambrose, both in its quantitative and in its rhythmical form, became a standard for poetry of all types, appearing even in the modern age as the long meter of the metrical versions of the Psalms. Trochaic verse, initiated in hymns by Hilary, employed most effectively by Fortunatus and always a favorite, rivalled the iambic in the vernaculars. As the metrical features of the Victorine sequence became increasingly popular, they were taken over bodily by secular poets writing both in Latin and in the modern European languages. Classical meters fostered by Prudentius and later by the Carolingian poets showed less vitality as poetical models. The liturgical hymn and the sequence are of prime importance in their metrical aspects but the meters of the *piae cantiones* and other religious lyrics were also widely appropriated. The origin of rhyme is a related problem which in the opinion of W. B. Sedgwick "centers around the Christian hymn."[1] Numerous publications by scholars who, like Sedgwick, have spoken with authority, bear witness to the general linguistic and literary interest attaching to these subjects of research.

Aside from aspects of meter and rhyme, medieval secular verse in Latin borrowed generously from the hymn; witness the songs of the wandering scholars as recorded in the collection edited under the title *Cambridge Songs* and also the goliardic poetry of the *Carmina Burana.*[2] Well-known hymns are frequently parodied and, in general, the liturgical models are employed to create humorous allusion or pungent satire. The student song *Gaudeamus igitur* is a familiar illustration of this general group.

The adaptation of the sequence to secular purposes resulted in a novel type of verse, the *modus*, already cited in connection with the origin of the sequence, illustrated by the *Modus florum* of which many examples have been preserved varying in beauty and poetic conceit. Reference has been made in an earlier chapter to the deeper problems underlying sequence origins on the poetical side. Discussion among scholars as to the priority of the religious or secular Latin lyric is still active.[3] Some would say that popular Latin verse arose by virtue of the hymnodic influence. Others would posit a vernacular impulse which eventuated in the Latin lyric both secular and religious.[4]

Apart from the lyric, there are in the general field of Latin verse many resemblances to hymnic models. The lengthy narrative poems of the *Peristephanon* in which Prudentius recounted the sufferings of the martyrs, St. Laurence, St. Vincent, St. Agnes, St. Eulalia and others, and celebrated their spiritual victories, have been called hymns. It has been argued that they were actually sung,[5] in full, upon the festival days of the saints in question although the praises of St. Vincent, for example, are expanded to 576 lines, other hymns varying from 66 to 1140 lines. It may have been possible in the more leisurely tempo of medieval life to render the martyr hymns of Prudentius in their entirety. A far more provocative suggestion makes them the starting point for the medieval saints' legend of which illustrations exist in lengthy Latin poems and later, in vernacular verse.

The contribution of hymns to the liturgical drama of the Church has been noted in connection with the sequence, *Victimae paschali laudes.* It is nowhere contended that the hymn created the drama but that the dramatic phraseology is often reminiscent of the hymn and that the role of the singers in the *schola cantorum* and the choir, as actors in the liturgical play, becomes significant in connection with the hymnic origins of these productions within the church.[6]

Finally, an interesting group of Latin poems having an interrelation with the hymn is illustrated by *O Roma nobilis*, a tenth century lyric praising the apostles and martyrs of the Eternal City (*A. H.* 51. 219).[7]

The transition from Latin to vernacular languages took place as soon as the latter were sufficiently developed to produce Christian verse. The Gospels were rendered into Germanic rhymed verse in the ninth century by Otfried the Frank who inserted a hymn of ten stanzas as a poetic version of the opening of St. John's Gospel. It is written in seven-syllable couplets with four or six to a stanza.[8] Otfried is said to have been influenced by Rabanus Maurus and with good reason since the latter was a recognized leader in mediating Latin patristic and other writings to the Germanic world of his day.

Otfried was the first of many medieval poets whose religious lyrics in the vernacular, often revealing the inspiration of the Latin hymn, have been preserved. Their verse appears in Wackernagel's great collection in which he has edited 1448 specimens from the time of Otfried to that of Hans Sachs.[9]

Celtic churchmen were pioneers among medieval Latin hymnists, their earliest contribution dating from the sixth century. Religious lyrics in the Celtic tongue must have been produced and recorded before the Danish invasions although the destruction of these manuscripts delayed the compiling of new vernacular collections until the eleventh century. The hymn *Hymnum dicat turba fratrum*, written in trochaic tetrameter, and preserved in the Bangor Antiphonary, to which reference has been made in Chapter One, apparently influenced the metrical system of Celtic poetry. The metrical pattern used by Otfried, a quatrain of seven-syllable lines with rhymed couplets, is commonly found.[10] Latin influence is at least tentatively acknowledged by scholars in the rhyme and stanza structure of Celtic poetry prior to the eleventh century.[11]

After the creation of the Latin sequence, vernacular poetry is overwhelmingly affected by this new type of hymn. Germanic poets followed the leadership of Notker. The Victorine school, rejecting the strophic system and rhythmic model of the Germans, built the couplet and rhyme, already existing in hymns, into a characteristic structure which proved to be easily transferable to vernacular uses. It has been asserted that the lyric poetry of the Middle Ages, in German, French, Provençal and English was reborn in this conquest of the vernacular by the Latin sequence.[12] At the same time, the possible influence of the vernacular over the Latin must not be ignored. There is a resemblance, for instance, between the narrative elements of sequences written in honor of saints and the ballads of secular poetry.[13] Whatever the conflicting currents may have been in the period of origins, the smooth-flowing stream of the vernacular religious lyric with its many tributaries, refreshed the spirit of medieval man and recalled to memory his religious heritage.

The vitality of this new religious poetry which flourishes in the later centuries, in which the Latin hymn suffered so marked a deterioration, suggests that the future of the hymn, like other media of Latin literature, was to be realized in a new linguistic environment. It was not the verity but the language that was destined to change.

In order to appreciate the variety and interest of that vernacular lyric poetry which arose within the sphere of influence of the Latin hymn, illustrations may be culled from many parts of Europe. *Mary-Verse in Meistergesang* is the title chosen by Sister Mary Schroeder for her study of one aspect of the German lyric.[14] A very large proportion, perhaps two-thirds of the songs are religious in content, showing to a degree, their dependence upon hymnal poetry, while nearly one-fourth of them are devoted to the praise of the Virgin. Occasionally, a Latin sequence has been freely translated, paraphrased or elaborated.

The Swedish vernacular is represented by the patriotic poem of Bishop Thomas of Strängnäs, who, in the fourteenth century, wrote in praise of the national hero, Engelbrekt. Metrical and stanza form are both of the hymnal type.[15]

The Romance languages afford myriad examples of the sequence form. St. Martial, near Limoges, already cited as a center in the production of the sequence, and Paris, the home of the Victorine school, are both places of origin for vernacular lyrics. A close connection has been traced between the sequence and the French romantic lyric, especially the *lai*, a connection amply illustrated and tabulated for the convenience of the student.[16] More familiar, perhaps, than the *lais* are the appealing lines of François Villon, "Dame des cieulx, regente terrienne," which possesses all the charm of the Marian lyric at its best.

About the year 1270, Alfonso X of Castile made a collection of 400 poems in the Galician-Portuguese dialect, the *Cántigas de Santa María* around which a considerable literature has grown up. All are devotional in subject matter. Alfonso X was a literary patron. Ramon Lull (c. 1315) was himself a poet who wrote in the Catalan tongue although his mystical writings are better known than his poetry. His *Hours of our Lady St. Mary* was modeled upon the hymn and set to a hymn tune.[17]

The Italian poets of religious verse flourished as writers both in the vernacular and in Latin. St. Francis of Assisi, (1181-1226), whose *Cantico di fratre sole*[18] is known and loved by countless persons in our own day, was among the earliest poets of the *Laudi spirituali*. The origin of the *laudi* has been traced in part to the ejaculations of the flagellants of northern Italy where bands of these penitents were commonly seen in the thirteenth century. A century earlier, religious societies of singers, the *laudisti*, were in existence in Venice and Florence. Arezzo knew such a group as early as 1068.[19] Included among the known writers of *laudi* are Jacopone da Todi, (1230-1306), and Bianco da Siena, (c. 1307), both classified today as writers of hymns.

The movement represented by the *laudisti* spread to France, German-speaking lands, the Low Countries and Poland. Everywhere the vernacular was used with popular unison melodies. As we approach the Renaissance, Florence is still conspicuous for her authors of the religious vernacular lyric, among them Lorenzo di Medici and Savonarola, (1452-1498), better known as the Florentine preacher whose passionate denunciations of the evils of his day brought him into conflict with the Church and resulted in his execution. His *Laude al crucifisso* has been translated in part by Jane F. Wilde as a hymn, "Jesus, refuge of the weary."

The English religious lyrics of the thirteenth, fourteenth and fifteenth centuries may be read with enjoyment in the collections of Carleton Brown whose appraisement of this poetry was the fruit of great learning and a sympathetic discernment of human values.[20] Here the Latin hymn may be found as it was translated, adapted and imitated in English verse. The Latin sequence, as it increased in popularity, was taken over by English poets with great success. Some of these writers who appropriated the Latin models, like William Herebert, Jacob Ryman and John Lydgate, are known to us by name while others are anonymous. Their poetic themes are varied but Marian verse appears in many forms: hymns, laments, and rhymed petition. Incidentally, a knowledge of the Latin original must be presupposed on the part of the English laity of this period. Chaucer wrote for the layman who must have understood his use of the sequence *Angelus ad Virginem* in the "Miller's Tale" and the sequence *Alma redemptoris mater* in the "Prioress' Tale."

English macaronic verse best reveals the Latin hymn. Over and over again, Latin quotations are used, sometimes embedded in the text, sometimes added as refrains, an understanding of which is always vital to the appreciation of the poem.

The carol, although extraneous to true hymnody, because of its nonliturgical character and usage, was related to Latin origins; to some extent, to the *cantio* and the *conductus*. A form of vernacular lyric, the carol often shares the macaronic features which were common in the blended phraseology of the European languages with Latin in this popular type of late medieval verse. It is relevant here as a religious lyric which bears the unmistakable mark of the hymnic inheritance. Whatever is true of the English carol is equally true of the carol in other lands. To-day these lyrics are of great interest and of increasing usage in the Christian Church at large. Their musical and poetic aspects are both subjects of enthusiastic research. Many persons in our modern society who have never studied the classical languages are able to sing the Latin words and phrases they contain, with understanding, as did their medieval predecessors.

II. Influence and Survival of Latin Hymns since the Middle Ages

The writing of Latin hymns by no means died out with the medieval era in the sixteenth century. The great prestige of Latin studies fostered by the Renaissance alone would have been sufficient to perpetuate the practice. The Church, too, was engaged in a movement to standardize and improve the Latinity of the breviary hymns which resulted in the Trentine cycle as we know it today. A concurrent movement toward uniformity of rites appreciably reduced the number of breviaries and the variety of their hymns, but those breviaries which maintained an independent existence had their own complete cycles. Such were the Cluniac Breviary of 1686 and the Paris Breviary of 1736 for which new hymns were written and sung side by side with those of medieval origin. Among post-Renaissance poets represented in these collections were the Frenchmen Jean-Baptiste de Santuil and his brothers Claude and Baptiste. Freshly inspired by classical studies, the new hymn writers repudiated medieval ruggedness and stylistic neglect in favor of the smooth and finished Latinity affected by contemporary poets. From the substantial body of verse produced in these centuries, *Adeste fideles*, "O come, all ye faithful," has proved a favorite. Sometimes classified as a hymn, sometimes as a carol, it originated in the English colony at Douay about the year 1740, from the pen of John Francis Wade.[21]

The continuity of the Roman Use, however, was not disturbed. The Roman Breviary had acquired its cycle of hymns in the processes of evolution which have been traced in the preceding chapters. Trentine revisions under the guidance of Pope Urban VIII, (1623-1644), made with the highest motives but often deplored by later scholars, transformed the medieval originals into products of the Renaissance. The Trentine Breviary contains many of the finest medieval hymns which, although they have suffered alterations, have carried the traditional heritage into modern times.[22]

By virtue of its prestige and its world-wide circulation, the Roman Breviary has been the vehicle by which the Latin hymn has penetrated into the modern vernacular languages in translations. It is a subject of frequent comment that the full treasury of hymns has not been drawn upon by the Catholic Church since the hymns of the Roman Breviary have monopolized the field. The historical reason for this is clear and also for the fact that in the Roman Missal only five sequences, each of recognized superiority, have been retained.

The restriction of Latin hymns in Roman Catholic liturgical usage to a relatively small number allows certain exceptions. The Benedictine and other religious orders use their own cycle of breviary hymns and present-day Catholic hymnals in popular use often contain translations of hymns and sequences additional to those of the Roman Breviary and Missal.

Protestant Churches are not limited in their selection of Latin hymns for translation, making their choices from the entire medieval store. The revival of Latin hymns in a translated form, which marked the Oxford Movement in the Anglican Church in the mid-nineteenth century, drew upon the Sarum Breviary as one native to English soil and therefore appropriate to the English Church. That these hymns were largely represented in the Roman Breviary, was well-known but the earlier and unrevised texts were preferred. In his function as a translator, John Mason Neale was preeminently a leader in the task of making known to the adherents of the Church of England their heritage of hymns.

An attempt was made at this time to perpetuate not only the words but the Gregorian Chant as a suitable musical setting for the vernacular. Here the innovators were only partly successful and the chant, although enthusiastically employed at first was gradually abandoned in the English Church as the sole musical vehicle for the Latin hymn in translation. Similarly Latin hymns have been taken over into other modern languages by translators of Protestant as well as Catholic allegiance.

In the seventeenth and eighteenth centuries the influence of Latin hymn meters continued to be felt in vernacular hymnody. Metrical versions of the Psalms made by Isaac Watts are often illustrative of old Latin forms which may also be recognized in his own hymns. This may not have been a conscious imitation of Latin originals for by this time hymn meters were ingrained in English poetry, but merely an indirect reflection, for example, of the Ambrosian model.

More subtle has been the influence in modern times of the most ancient canons of hymnic expression; objective presentation of scriptural narrative, doctrinal emphasis and a certain joyful austerity in the praise of God. During the three and a half centuries which have passed since the era of the Protestant Reformation, the Christian hymn has experienced a succession of literary movements, reflecting, for example, the spirit of the Age of Reason and of the Romantic Era. Contemporary musical evolution has, in turn, been vitally important to the growth of the hymn as it has been mated with the melodies of the Genevan Psalter, the chorales of Bach, the musical novelties of instrumental origin, the folk song and latterly the native music of regions open to missionary enterprise.

Throughout this varied experience the stream of medieval Latin hymnody has continued its course. As an accompaniment of Roman Catholic worship this was only to be expected. The conquest by the Latin hymn of areas beyond the limits of the Roman Church is more significant. The most recent hymnals of leading Protestant denominations, to which the Latin hymn in translation has made a modest but genuine contribution, bear witness to the ageless character of this hymnody. Modern investigation of hymn sources, their origins, authorship and influence, has created the study of documentary hymnology as it is known today. In the processes of this inquiry the medieval Latin hymn has been invested with new interest in the minds of a multitude of worshipers, both Catholic and Protestant, who have hitherto been unaware of, or indifferent to, their common heritage.

Illustrative Hymns

I. *Splendor paternae gloriae*

1. Splendor paternae gloriae, De luce lucem proferens, Lux lucis et fons luminis, Dies dierum illuminans,	1. O Splendor of God's glory bright, O Thou that bringest light from light, O Light of light, light's living spring, O Day, all days illumining;
2. Verusque sol illabere, Micans nitore perpeti, Iubarque sancti Spiritus Infunde nostris sensibus.	2. O Thou true Sun, on us thy glance Let fall in royal radiance, The Spirit's sanctifying beam Upon our earthly senses stream.
3. Votis vocemus et Patrem – Patrem perennis gloriae, Patrem potentis gratiae – Culpam releget lubricam,	3. The Father, too, our prayers implore, Father of glory evermore, The Father of all grace and might, To banish sin from our delight:
4. Informet actus strenuos, Dentem retundat invidi, Casus secundet asperos, Donet gerendi gratiam.	4. To guide whate'er we nobly do, With love all envy to subdue, To make all-fortune turn to fair, And give us grace our wrongs to bear.
5. Mentem gubernet et regat, Casto fideli corpore; Fides calore ferveat, Fraudis venena nesciat.	5. Our mind be in his keeping placed, Our body true to him and chaste, Where only Faith her fire shall feed To burn the tares of Satan's seed.
6. Christusque nobis sit cibus, Potusque noster sit fides; Laeti bibamus sobriam Ebrietatem Spiritus.	6. And Christ to us for food shall be, From him our drink that welleth free, The Spirit's wine, that maketh whole, And mocking not, exalts the soul.
7. Laetus dies hic transeat, Pudor sit ut diluculum, Fides velut meridies, Crepusculum mens nesciat.	7. Rejoicing may this day go hence, Like virgin dawn our innocence. Like fiery noon our faith appear, Nor know the gloom of twilight drear.

8. Aurora cursus provehit, Aurora totus prodeat, In Patre totus Filius, Et totus in Verbo Pater.	8. Morn in her rosy car is borne; Let Him come forth our perfect Morn, The Word in God the Father one, The Father perfect in the Son.

Tr. Robert Bridges, from *The Yattendon Hymnal* (edited by Robert Bridges & H. Ellis Wooldridge) by permission of the Clarendon Press, Oxford.

II. *Vexilla regis prodeunt*

1. Vexilla regis prodeunt, Fulget crucis mysterium, Quo carne carnis conditor Suspensus est patibulo.	1. The banners of the king advance, The cross with mystery doth flame, And from the tree the Flesh of flesh, Word Incarnate, hangs in shame.
2. Quo vulneratus insuper Mucrone dirae lanceae, Ut nos lavaret crimine, Manavit unda, sanguine.	2. The lance's edge hath pierced His side, O look on Him that for our good Cleansed us of the stain of sin, Washed out with water and with blood
3. Inpleta sunt quae concinit David fideli carmine, Dicendo nationibus: Regnavit a ligno Deus.	3. Now is fulfilled what was foretold By David in prophetic song: Suspended from the rood Our God Will rule. To Him shall nations throng.
4. Arbor decora et fulgida, Ornata regis purpura, Electa digno stipite Tam sancta membra tangere.	4. O glorious and radiant tree In royal crimson richly decked, His sacred limbs to touch and hold Thee did our Lord, fair rood, elect.
5. Beata, cuius bracchiis Pretium pependit saeculi. Statera facta est corporis Praedam tulitque tartari.	5. Thou blessed cross upon whose arms The body of the Savior fell; As with a balance thou didst weigh The Christ that bore us out of Hell.

6. Fundis aroma cortice,
Vincis sapore nectare,
Iocunda fructu fertili
Plaudis triumpho nobili.

6. Thy wood is all a sweet perfume,
Thou art like nectar very sweet;
Rejoicing in thy fruit thou mak'st
A perfect triumph more complete.

7. Salve ara, salve victima
De passionis gloria,
Qua vita mortem pertulit
Et morte vitam reddidit.

7. Altar and sacred victim, hail!
In thy passion is our glory.
Life from death thou bringest back,
Life in death shall be our story.

8. O crux ave, spes unica,
Hoc passionis tempore,
Auge piis iustitiam,
Reisque dona veniam.

8. Hail thou cross, O hail thou only
Hope that agony may win;
To believers bring salvation,
Take the sinner from his sin!

The 8th stanza is a later addition. Stanza 2 omitted.

Tr. Howard M. Jones (Allen, P. S., *The Romanesque Lyric*. Chapel Hill, Un. of N. C. Press, 1928, p. 146-7. Quoted by permission of publishers.)

III. *Aeterna Christi munera*

1. Aeterna Christi munera
Et martyrum victorias,
Laudes ferentes debitas
Laetis canamus mentibus.

1. The eternal gifts of Christ the King,
The Martyrs' glorious deeds we sing;
And while due hymns of praise we pay,
Our thankful hearts cast grief away.

2. Ecclesiarum principes,
Belli triumphales duces,
Caelestis aulae milites,
Et vera mundi lumina;

2. The Church in these her princes boasts,
These victor chiefs of warrior hosts;
The soldiers of the heavenly hall,
The lights that rose on earth for all.

3. Terrore victo saeculi,
Poenisque spretis corporis,
Mortis sacrae compendio
Vitam beatam possident.

3. The terrors of the world despised,
The body's torments lightly prized,
By one brief space of death and pain
Life everlasting they obtain.

4. Traduntur igni martyres
Et bestiarum dentibus;
Armata saevit ungulis
Tortoris insani manus.

4. To flames the Marytr Saints are hailed:
By teeth of savage beasts assailed;
Against them, armed with ruthless brand
And hooks of steel, their torturers stand.

5. Nudata pendent viscera,
Sanguis sacratus funditur,
Sed permanent immobiles
Vitae perennis gratia.

5. The mangled frame is tortured sore,
The holy life-drops freshly pour:
They stand unmoved amidst the strife,
By grace of everlasting life.

6. Devota sanctorum fides,
Invicta spes credentium,
Perfecta Christi caritas
Mundi triumphat principem.

6. 'Twas thus the yearning faith of saints,
The unconquered hope that never faints,
The love of Christ that knows not shame,
The Prince of this world overcame.

7. In his paterna gloria,
In his voluntas filii,
Exultat in his spiritus;
Caelum repletur gaudiis.

7. In these the Father's glory shone;
In these the will of God the Son;
In these exults the Holy Ghost;
Through these rejoice the heavenly host.

8. Te nunc, Redemptor, quaesumus,
Ut ipsorum consortio
Iungas precantes servulos
In sempiterna saecula.

8. Redeemer, hear us of thy love,
That, with the glorious band above,
Hereafter, of thine endless grace,
Thy servants also may have place.

Tr. John Mason Neale, *Hymnal Noted.*

IV. *Nocte surgentes vigilemus omnes*

1. Nocte surgentes, vigilemus omnes,
Semper in psalmis meditemur, atque
Viribus totis Domino canamus
Dulciter hymnos,

1. Father, we praise thee, now the night is over,
Active and watchful, stand we all before thee;
Singing we offer prayer and meditation:
Thus we adore thee.

2. Ut pio regi pariter canentes
Cum suis sanctis mereamur aulam
Ingredi caeli, simul et beatam
Ducere vitam.

2. Monarch of all things, fit us for thy mansions;
Banish our weakness, health and wholeness sending;
Bring us to heaven, where thy Saints united
Joy without ending.

3. Praestet hoc nobis Deitas beata
Patris ac Nati pariterque sancti
Spiritus, cuius reboatur omni
Gloria mundo.

3. All-holy Father, Son and equal Spirit,
Trinity blessed, send us thy salvation;
Thine is the glory, gleaming and resounding
Through all creation.

Tr. Percy Dearmer, from *The English Hymnal* by permission of the Oxford University Press.

V. *Alleluia*

1. Alleluia piis edite laudibus,
Cives aetherei, psallite naviter
Alleluia perenne.

1. Sing alleluia forth in duteous praise,
Ye citizens of heav'n; O sweetly raise
An endless alleluia.

2. Hinc vos perpetui luminis accola,
Assumet resonans hymniferis choris,
Alleluia perenne.

2. Ye powers who stand before th' Eternal Light,
In hymning choirs re-echo to the height
An endless alleluia.

3. Vos urbs eximia suscipiet Dei,
Quae laetis resonans cantibus excitat
Alleluia perenne.

3. The Holy City shall take up your strain,
And with glad songs resounding wake again
An endless alleluia.

4. Felici reditu gaudia sumite
Reddentes Domino glorificos melos,
Alleluia perenne.

4. In blissful antiphons ye thus rejoice
To render to the Lord with thankful voice
An endless alleluia.

5. Almum sidereae iam patriae decus
Victores capitis, quo canor est iugis
Alleluia perenne.

5. Ye who have gained at length your palms in bliss,
Victorious ones, your chant shall still be this,
An endless alleluia.

6. Illic regis honor vocibus inclitis
Iucunda reboat carmina perpetim
Alleluia perenne.

6. There, in one glad acclaim, forever ring
The strains which tell the honour of your king,
An endless alleluia.

Stanzas 7, 8, 9 omitted.
Tr. John Ellerton

VI. *Sancti venite*

1. Sancti venite, Christi corpus sumite,
Sanctum bibentes, quo redempti sanguinem.

1. Draw nigh, and take the Body of the Lord,
And drink the Holy Blood for you outpoured.

2. Salvati Christi corpore et sanguine,
A quo refecti laudes dicamus Deo.

2. Saved by that Body, hallowed by that Blood,
Whereby refreshed, we render thanks to God.

3. Hoc sacramento corporis et sanguinis
Omnes exuti ab inferni faucibus.

4. Dator salutis, Christus filius Dei,
Mundum salvavit per crucem et sanguinem.

3.* Salvation's Giver, Christ the Only Son;
By that His Cross and Blood the victory won.

5. Pro universis immolatus Dominus
Ipse sacerdos exstitit et hostia.

4. Offered was He for greatest and for least:
Himself the Victim, and Himself the Priest.

6. Lege praeceptum immolari hostias,
Qua adumbrantur divina mysteria.

5. Victims were offered by the Law of old,
That, in a type, celestial mysteries told.

7. Lucis indultor et salvator omnium
Praeclaram sanctis largitus est gratiam.

6. He, Ransomer from death and Light from shade,
Giveth His holy grace His Saints to aid.

8. Accedant omnes pura mente creduli,
Sumant aeternam salutis custodiam.

7. Approach ye then with faithful hearts sincere,
And take the safeguard of salvation here.

9. Sanctorum custos, rector quoque, Dominus,
Vitae perennis largitor credentibus.

8. He That in this world rules His Saints, and shields,
To all believers Life Eternal yields:

10. Caelestem panem dat esurientibus,
De fonte vivo praebet sitientibus.

9. With Heavenly Bread makes them that hunger whole;
Gives Living Waters to the thirsty soul.

11. Alpha et omega ipse Christus Dominus Venit, venturus iudicare homines.	10. Alpha and Omega, to Whom shall bow All nations at the Doom, is with us now.

Tr. John Mason Neale, *Mediaeval Hymns and Sequences*, London. Masters, 1867, p. 13.
*Neale omits Latin stanza 3.

VII. *Ave maris stella*

1. Ave maris stella, Dei mater alma Atque semper virgo, Felix caeli porta.	1. Hail, Sea-star we name thee, Ever-maid acclaim thee, God His Mother, Portal To the life immortal.
2. Sumens illud Ave Gabrielis ore Funda nos in pace, Mutans nomen Evae.	2. Ave was the token By the Angel spoken: Peace on earth it telleth, Eva's name re-spelleth.
3. Solve vincla reis, Profer lumen caecis, Mala nostra pelle, Bona cuncta posce.	3. Free the worldly-minded Luminate the blinded, Every ill repressing, Win us every blessing.
4. Monstra te esse matrem, Sumat per te preces, Qui pro nobis natus Tulit esse tuus.	4. Plead, and play the Mother! He will, and no other, Born for our salvation, Hear thy supplication.
5. Virgo singularis, Inter omnes mitis, Nos culpis solutos Mites fac et castos.	5. Maiden meek and lowly, Singularly holy, Loose the sins that chain us; Sanctify, sustain us.

6. Vitam praesta puram, Iter para tutum, Ut videntes Iesum Semper collaetemur.	6. Help us live in pureness, Smooth our way with sureness, Till we also eye Thee, Jesu, ever nigh Thee.
7. Sit laus Deo Patri, Summo Christo decus, Spiritui Sancto: Tribus honor unus.	7. Doxology.

Tr. G. R. Woodward

VIII. *Ut queant laxis resonare fibris*

(St. John the Baptist)

1. Ut queant laxis resonare fibris Mira gestorum famuli tuorum, Solve polluti labii reatum, Sancte Ioannes.	1. In flowing measures worthily to sing The wonders which of old by thee were done, To lips unclean let Heaven remission bring, O Holy John!
2. Nuntius celso veniens Olympo, Te patri magnum fore nasciturum, Nomen et vitae seriem gerendae Ordine promit.	2. From highest Heaven a herald sent to earth Thy future greatness to thy father told; Thy name and life in order from thy birth Entire unrolled.
3. Ille promissi dubius superni, Perdidit promptae modulos loquelae, Sed reformasti genitus peremptae Organa vocis	3. Yet doubting of the promise of his Lord His palsied tongue of language lost the power; By thee was all his faltering speech restored Thy natal hour.

4. Ventris obtruso recubans cubili, Senseras regem thalamo manentem, Hinc parens nati meritis uterque Abdita pandit.	4. Thou didst within the narrow womb discern The King in that his chamber lie concealed; Each parent her Son's dignity in turn To each revealed.
5. Sit decus Patri, genitaeque Proli, Et tibi, compar utriusque virtus, Spiritus semper, Deus unus, omni Temporis aevo.	5. Now whilst Heaven's citizens proclaim thy praise God ever One and yet coequal Three For pardon we our suppliant voices raise Redeemed by Thee!

Tr. J. D. Chambers. Stanzas 6-13 omitted.

IX. *Veni creator spiritus*

1. Veni creator Spiritus Mentes tuorum visita, Imple superna gratia, Quae tu creasti pectora.	1. Creator-spirit, all-Divine, Come, visit every soul of thine, And fill with thy celestial flame The hearts which thou thyself didst frame.
2. Qui Paraclitus diceris, Donum Dei altissimi, Fons vivus, ignis, caritas, Et spiritalis unctio.	2. O gift of God, thine is the sweet Consoling name of Paraclete– And spring of life and fire and love And unction flowing from above.
3. Tu septiformis munere, Dextrae Dei tu digitus, Tu rite promisso Patris Sermone ditas guttura.	3. The mystic sevenfold gifts are thine, Finger of God's right hand divine; The Father's promise sent to teach The tongue a rich and heavenly speech.
4. Accende lumen sensibus, Infunde amorem cordibus, Infirma nostri corporis Virtute firmans perpeti.	4. Kindle with fire brought from above Each sense, and fill our hearts with love; And grant our flesh, so weak and frail, The strength of thine which cannot fail.

5. Hostem repellas longius,
Pacemque dones protinus,
Ductore sic te praevio
Vitemus omne noxium.

5. Drive far away our deadly foe,
And grant us thy true peace to know;
So we, led by thy guidance still,
May safely pass through every ill.

6. Da gaudiorum praemia,
Da gratiarum munera,
Dissolve litis vincula,
Adstringe pacis foedera.

6. To us, through Thee, the grace be shown
To know the Father and the Son;
And Spirit of them both, may we
Forever rest our faith in Thee.

7. Per te sciamus, da, Patrem,
Noscamus atque Filium,
Te utriusque Spiritum
Credamus omni tempore.

7. To Sire and Son be praises meet,
And to the Holy Paraclete;
And may Christ send us from above
That Holy Spirit's gift of love.

8. Sit laus Patri cum Filio,
Sancto simul Paraclito,
Nobisque mittat Filius
Charisma sancti Spiritus.

Tr. J. A. Aylward

X. *Deus immensa trinitas*

(Mozarabic, Common of Saints)

1. Deus, immensa trinitas,
Unita semper gloria,
Pater, Christe, Paraclite,
Rerum invicte Domine.

1. O glorious immensity
And one eternal Trinity,
Father and Comforter and Word,
Of all that is, unconquered Lord,

2. Qui largitatem muneris
Quo praestasti martyri,
Cuius festa votissima,
Quam celebramus hodie.

2. The saint for whom our chants of praise
Consenting on this feast we raise,
With princely guerdons thou didst bless:
Thy crown, thy palm, thy happiness.

3. Tormenta qui saevissima
Ac varia supplicia
Victrice tua dextera
Mente robusta pertulit.

3. In tortures, great and cruel pain
Thou didst with thy right hand sustain
Thy servant, who with steadfast heart
Bore the tormentor's every art.

4. Huius, adclines, Domine,
Te deprecamur, precibus,
Aetherea consortia,
Celsa dona fastigia.

4. Thy gracious ear, O Christ divine,
Unto thy servant's prayer incline,
To whom thy fairest gifts are given
Within the gracious halls of heaven.

5. Qui princeps esse principum
Rex mysticus agnosceris,
Agnita nostra crimina
Large dele clementia.

5. Thee Prince of Princes, we proclaim,
The King that bears the mystic name:
Blot out in thy great love, we pray,
The sins that mar this holy day.

6. Adventus ut cum fulgidus
Tuus, Christe, patuerit,
Tuo ducante martyre
Laeti pergamus obviam.

6. That so when Thou shalt come again,
O Christ, in light, on earth to reign,
Led by thy martyr, we may dare
To rise to meet thee in the air.

7. (added)
Deo Patri sit gloria
Eiusque soli Filio
Cum Spiritu Paraclito
Et nunc et omne saeculum.

7. (added)
To God the Father glory be,
And God the Son eternally,
With God the Holy Paraclete
Through endless ages, as is meet.

Tr. Alan G. Mcdougall (*Pange Lingua etc.*, Burns, Oates & Washbourne, London, 1916. p. 71. Quoted by permission of publishers.)

XI. *Sancti spiritus assit nobis gratia*

1. Sancti spiritus assit nobis gratia,

1. The grace of the Holy Ghost be present with us;

2. Quae corda nostra sibi faciat habitaculum

2. And make our hearts a dwelling place to itself;

3. Expulsis inde cunctis vitiis spiritalibus.	3. And expel from them all spiritual wickedness.
4. Spiritus alme, illustrator hominum,	4. Merciful Spirit, Illuminator of men,
5. Horridas nostrate mentis purga tenebras.	5. Purge the fearful shades of our mind.
6. Amator sancte sensatorum semper cogitatuum,	6. O holy Lover of thoughts that are ever wise,
7. Infunde unctionem tuam clemens nostris sensibus.	7. Of Thy mercy pour forth Thine Anointing into our senses.
8. Tu purificator omnium flagitiorum spiritus,	8. Thou purifier of all iniquities, O Spirit,
9. Purifica nostri oculum interioris hominis,	9. Purify the eye of our inner man,
10. Ut videri supremus genitor possit a nobis,	10. To the end that the Father of all things may be seen by us,
11. Mundi cordis quem soli cernere possunt oculi.	11. He, Whom the eyes of none save the pure in heart can behold.
12. Prophetas tu inspirasti, ut praeconia Christi praecinuissent inclita;	12. Thou didst inspire the Prophets to chant aforehand their glorious heralding of Christ.
13. Apostolos confortasti, uti tropaeum Christi per totum mundum veherent.	13. Thou didst confirm the Apostles, so that they shall bear Christ's glorious trophy through the whole world.

14. Quando machinam per verbum suum fecit Deus caeli, terrae, marium,	14. When by His Word, God made the system of heaven, earth, seas,
15. Tu super aquas foturus eas numen tuum expandisti, spiritus.	15. Thou didst stretch out Thy Godhead over the waters, and didst cherish them, O Spirit!
16. Tu animabus vivificandis aquas fecundas;	16. Thou didst give virtue to the waters to quicken souls;
17. Tu aspirando das spiritales esse homines.	17. Thou, by Thine Inspiration, grantest to men to be spiritual.
18. Tu divisum per linguas mundum et ritus adunasti, Domine;	18. Thou didst unite the world, divided into tongues and rites, O Lord!
19. Idolatras ad cultum Dei revocas, magistrorum optime.	19. Thou recallest idolaters to the worship of God, best of Masters!
20. Ergo nos supplicantes tibi exaudi propitius, sancte spiritus,	20. Wherefore of Thy mercy hear us who call upon Thee, Holy Ghost:
21. Sine quo preces omnes cassae creduntur et indignae Dei auribus.	21. Without Whom, as the faith teaches, all our prayers are in vain, and unworthy of the ears of God,
22. Tu, qui omnium saeculorum sanctos Tui numinis docuisti instinctu amplectendo, spiritus,	22. Thou, O Spirit, who by embracing the Saints of all ages, dost teach them by the impulse of Thy Divinity;

23. Ipse hodie apostolos Christi donans munere insolito et cunctis inaudito saeculis	23. Thyself, by bestowing upon the Apostles of Christ a gift immortal, and unheard of from all ages,
24. Hunc diem gloriosum fecisti.	24. Hast made this day glorious.

Tr. John Mason Neale, *Mediaeval Hymns and Sequences,* London. Masters, 1867, p. 29.

XII. *Cantemus cuncti melodum nunc Alleluia*

1. Cantemus cuncti melodum nunc, *Alleluia.*	1. The strain upraise of joy and praise, Alleluia.
2. In laudibus aeterni regis haec plebs resultet *Alleluia.*	2. To the glory of their King Shall the ransomed people sing Alleluia.
3. Hoc denique caelestes chori cantant in altum *Alleluia.*	3. And the Choirs that dwell on high Shall re-echo through the sky Alleluia.
4. Hoc beatorum per prata paradisiaca psallat concentus *Alleluia.*	4. They through the fields of Paradise that roam, The blessed ones, repeat that bright home Alleluia.
5. Quin et astrorum micantia luminaria iubilant altum *Alleluia.*	5. The planets glitt'ring on their heavenly way, The shining constellations, join, and say Alleluia.
6. Nubium cursus, ventorum volatus, fulgurum coruscatio et tonitruum sonitus dulce consonent simul *Alleluia.*	6. Ye clouds that onward sweep! Ye winds on pinions light! Ye thunders, echoing loud and deep! Ye lightnings, wildly bright! In sweet consent unite your Alleluia.

7. Fluctus et undae, imber et procellae, tempestas et serenitas, cauma, gelu, nix, pruinae, saltus, nemora pangant *Alleluia.*	7. Ye floods and ocean billows! Ye storms and winter snow! Ye days of cloudless beauty! Hoar frost and summer glow! Ye groves that wave in spring, And glorious forests, sing Alleluia.
8. Hinc, variae volucres, creatorem laudibus concinite cum *Alleluia.*	8. First let the birds, with painted plummage gay, Exalt their great Creator's praise, and say Alleluia.
9. Ast illinc respondant voces altae diversarum bestiarum *Alleluia.*	9. Then let the beasts of earth, with varying strain, Join in Creation's Hymn, and cry again Alleluia.
10.* Istinc montium celsi vertices sonent *Alleluia.*	10.* Here let the mountains thunder forth, sonorous, Alleluia There let the valleys sing in gentler chorus, Alleluia.
11. Illinc vallium profunditates saltent *Alleluia.*	11. Thou jubilant abyss of ocean, cry Alleluia. Ye tracts of earth and continents, reply Alleluia.
12. Tu quoque, maris iubilans abysse, dic *Alleluia.*	12. To God, Who all Creation made, The frequent hymn be duly paid: Alleluia.
13. Necnon terrarum molis immensitates: *Alleluia.*	13. This is the strain, the eternal strain, the Lord of all things loves: Alleluia. This is the song, the heav'nly song, that Christ Himself approves: Alleluia.

14. Nunc omne genus
humanum laudans exsultet
Alleluia.

14. Wherefore we sing, both heart and voice
awaking, Alleluia.
And children's voices echo, answer
making, Alleluia.

15. Et creatori
grates frequentans consonet
Alleluia.

15. Now from all men be outpour'd
Alleluia to the Lord;
With Alleluia evermore
The Son and Spirit we adore.

16. Hoc denique nomen audire
iugiter delectatur
Alleluia.

16. Praise be done to the Three in One.
Alleluia! Alleluia! Alleluia! Alleluia!

17. Hoc etiam carmen caeleste
comprobat ipse Christus
Alleluia.

18. Nunc vos, O socii,
cantate laetantes
Alleluia.

19. Et vos, pueruli,
respondete semper
Alleluia.

20. Nunc omnes canite simul
Alleluia Domino,
Alleluia Christo
Pneumatique *Alleluia.*

21. Laus trinitati aeternae:
Alleluia, Alleluia,
Alleluia, Alleluia,
Alleluia, Alleluia.

Tr. John Mason Neale, *Mediaeval Hymns and Sequences*, London. Masters, 1867, p. 43.
*Stanzas 10-13 translate Latin 10-21.

XIII. *Heri mundus exultavit*

1. Heri mundus exultavit, Et exultans celebravit Christi natalitia: Heri chorus angelorum Prosecutus est caelorum Regem cum laetitia.	1. Yesterday, with exultation Joined the world in celebration Of her promis'd Saviour's birth; Yesterday the Angel nation Pour'd the strains of jubilation O'er the Monarch born on earth.
2. Protomartyr et Levita, Clarus fide, clarus vita, Clarus et miraculis, Sub hac luce triumphavit, Et triumphans insultavit Stephanus incredulis.	2. But to-day, o'er death victorious, By His faith and actions glorious, By His miracles renown'd, Dared the Deacon Protomartyr Earthly life for Heav'n to barter, Faithful midst the faithless found.
3. Fremunt ergo tanquam ferae, Quia victi defecere Lucis victi adversarii: Falsos testes statuunt, Et linguas exacuunt Viperarum filii.	*3. In a hopeless strife engaging, They like savage beasts are raging, Adversaries of the light; False the witnesses they set; Tongues like swords the rabble whet, Viper brood of darkest night.
4. Agonista, nulli cede; Certa certus de mercede, Perservera, Stephane: Insta falsis testibus, Confuta sermonibus Synagogam Satanae.	4. Forward, champion, in thy quarrel! Certain of a certain laurel, Holy Stephen, persevere! Perjur'd witnesses confounding Satan's Synagogue astounding By thy doctrine true and clear.
5. Testis tuus est in caelis, Testis verax et fidelis, Testis innocentiae. Nomen habes coronati, Te tormenta decet pati Pro corona gloriae.	5. Lo! in Heaven thy Witness liveth: Bright and faithful proof He giveth Of His Martyr's blamelessness: Thou by name a Crown impliest; Meetly then in pangs thou diest For the Crown of Righteousness!

6. Pro corona non marcenti Perfer brevis vim tormenti, Te manet victoria. Tibi fiet mors, natalis, Tibi poena terminalis Dat vitae primordia.	6. For a crown that fadeth never, Bear the torturer's brief endeavour; Victory waits to end the strife: Death shall be thy birth's beginning, And life's losing be the winning Of the true and better Life.
7. Plenus Sancto Spiritu Penetrat intuitu Stephanus caelestia. Videns Dei gloriam Crescit ad victoriam, Suspirat ad praemia.	7. Whom the Holy Ghost endueth. Whom celestial sight embueth, Stephen penetrates the skies; There God's fullest glory viewing There his victor strength renewing For his near reward he sighs.
8. En a dextris Dei stantem Iesum, pro te dimicantem, Stephane, considera. Tibi caelos reserari, Tibi Christum revelari Clama voce libera.	8. See, as Jewish foes invade thee, See how Jesus stands to aid thee! Stands to guard His champion's death: Cry that opened Heaven is shown thee: Cry that Jesus waits to own thee: Cry it with thy latest breath!
9. Se commendat Salvatori, Pro quo dulce ducit mori Sub ipsis lapidibus. Saulus servat omnium Vestes lapidantium, Lapidans in omnibus.	*9. On his Saviour's aid relying, Sweet to him the pain of dying, 'Neath the fearful rain of stone: Paul amidst the stoning throng, Guarding garments, makes the wrong Of the angry Jews his own.
10. Ne peccatum statuatur His, a quibus lapidatur, Genu ponit et precatur, Condolens insaniae: In Christo sic obdormivit, Qui Christo sic obedivit, Et cum Christo semper vivit, Martyrum primitiae.	10. As the dying Martyr kneeleth, For his murderers he appealeth, And his prayer their pardon sealeth, For their madness grieving sore; Then in Christ he sleepeth sweetly, Who His pattern kept completely, Martyr first-fruits, evermore!

Tr. John Mason Neale, *Mediaeval Hymns and Sequences,* London. Masters, 1867, p. 134.
*Tr. Stephen A. Hurlbut. Quoted by permission of author. Stanzas 11, 12 omitted.

XIV. *Ad perennis vitae fontem*

1. Ad perennis vitae fontem mens sitivit arida;
Claustra carnis praesto frangi clausa quaerit anima:
Gliscit, ambit, eluctatur exul frui patria.

1. To the fount of life eternal cries the soul with longing thirst,
And the spirit, flesh-imprisoned, seeks the bars of flesh to burst;
Strives to gain that heavenly country, exiled now and sin-accurst.

2. Dum pressuris ac aerumnis se gemit obnoxiam,
Quam amisit, dum deliquit, contemplatur gloriam,
Praesens malum auget boni perditi memoriam.

2. Sore beset with care and danger, groans the spirit for release,
Still beholds, though lost in Eden, glory forfeited and peace;
Former good, in memory dwelling, doth the present ill increase.

3. Nam quis promat summae pacis quanta sit laetitia,
Ubi vivis margaritis surgunt aedificia,
Auro celsa micant tecta, radiant triclinia?

3. Who can tell how great the joy of that Peace surpassing all,
Where of living pearls constructed rise the stately buildings tall,
Where with gold the rooftree glitters, shines with gold the banquet-hall.

4. Solis gemmis pretiosis haec structura nectitur;
Auro mundo, tamquam vitro, urbis via sternitur;
Abest limus, deest fimus, lues nulla cernitur.

4. All of precious stones compacted rise those structures of delight;
Purest gold as crystal shining paves the heavenly city bright;
Never mire nor filth defiling stains the streets of radiant light.

5. Hiems horrens, aestas torrens illic numquam saeviunt;
Flos perpetuus rosarum ver agit perpetuum;
Candent lilia, rubescit crocus, sudat balsamum.

5. Chilling winter, burning summer, neither rages in that land,
But the crimson bloom of roses doth an endless spring demand;
White the lilies, red the crocus, fragrant doth the balsam stand.

6. Virent prata, vernant sata, rivi mellis influunt;
Pigmentorum spirat odor, liquor et aromatum;
Pendent poma floridorum non lapsura nemorum.

6. Green the pastures, flower-besprinkled, fed by streams with honey filled;
All the air is sweet with incense from the odorous herbs distilled;
Never fails the ripened fruitage, nor is bloom by winter chilled.

7. Non alternat luna vices, sol, vel cursus siderum;
Agnus est felicis urbis lumen inocciduum;
Nox et tempus desunt ei, diem fert continuum.

7. Waxeth not the moon nor waneth, need not sun or stars to be,
But the Lamb in that blest city shines a Sun eternally;
There the daylight is unbroken, night and time have ceased to be.

8. Nam et sancti quique velut sol praeclarus rutilant;
Post triumphum coronati mutuo coniubilant,
Et prostrati pugnas hostis iam securi numerant.

8. Shine the blessed with a splendor like the splendor of the sun;
Crowned in triumph stand they singing that the race of life is run;
Now secure, they count the glories of the contest they have won.

9. Omni labe defaecati carnis bella nesciunt,
Caro facta spiritalis et mens unum sentiunt;
Pace multa perfruentes scandalum non perferunt.

9. Cleansed from every stain of evil, they from carnal strife are free;
Flesh made spirit, with the spirit doth for evermore agree,
There, released from all temptation, they shall Peace unbroken see.

. . . .

. . . .

20. Probes vires inexhausto laboranti proelio,
Nec quietem post procinctum deneges emerito,
Te que merear potiri sine fine praemio!

20. Strength supply, in heat or conflict, ceaseless struggle to maintain;
Grant thy servant, warfare ended, well-deserved rest to gain;
Grant that I, Thyself deserving, may Thyself as prize attain!

Tr. Stephen A. Hurlbut. Quoted by permission of author.

XV. *Lauda, Sion, Salvatorem*

1. Lauda, Sion, Salvatorem,
Lauda ducem et pastorum
In hymnis et canticis:
Quantum potes, tantum aude,
Quia maior omni laude,
Nec laudare sufficis.

1. Praise, O Sion, praise thy Saviour,
Shepherd, Prince, with glad behavior,
Praise in hymn and canticle:
Sing His glory without measure,
For the merit of your treasure
Never shall your praises fill.

2. Laudis thema specialis,
Panis vivus et vitalis
Hodie proponitur;
Quem in sacrae mensa cenae
Turbae fratrum duodenae
Datum non ambigitur.

2. Wondrous theme of mortal singing,
Living bread and bread life-bringing,
Sing we on this joyful day:
At the Lord's own table given
To the twelve as bread from heaven,
Doubting not we firmly say.

3. Sit laus plena, sit sonora
Sit iucunda, sit decora
Mentis iubilatio:
Namque dies est sollemnis
Qua recolitur perennis
Mensae institutio.

3. Sing His praise with voice sonorous;
Every heart shall hear the chorus
Swell in melody sublime:
For this day the Shepherd gave us
Flesh and blood to feed and save us,
Lasting to the end of time.

4. In hac mensa novi Regis
Novum pascha novae legis
Phase vetus terminat:
Iam vetustas novitati,
Umbra cedit veritati,
Noctem lux eliminat.

4. At the new King's sacred table,
The new law's new pasch is able
To succeed the ancient rite:
Old to new its place hath given,
Truth has far the shadows driven,
Darkness flees before the Light.

5. Quod in cena Christus gessit,
Faciendum hoc expressit
In sui memoriam:
Docti sacris institutis,
Panem, vinum in salutis
Conscramus hostiam.

5. And as He hath done and planned it—
"Do this"—hear His love command it,
"For a memory of me."
Learnèd, Lord, in thy own science,
Bread and wine, in sweet compliance,
As a Host we offer Thee.

6. Dogma datur Christianis,
Quod in carnem transit panis,
Et vinum in sanguinem:
Quod non capis, quod non vides,
Animosa firmat fides,
Praeter rerum ordinem.

6. Thus in faith the Christian heareth:
That Christ's flesh as bread appeareth,
And as wine His precious blood:
Though we feel it not nor see it,
Living faith that doth decree it
All defects of sense makes good.

7. Sub diversis speciebus,
Signis tamen et non rebus,
Latent res eximiae:
Caro cibus, sanguis potus,
Manet tamen Christus totus
Sub utraque specie.

7. Lo! beneath the species dual
(Signs not things), is hid a jewel
Far beyond creation's reach!
Though His flesh as food abideth,
And His blood as drink—He hideth
Undivided under each.

8. A sumente non concisus,
Non confractus, non divisus,
Integer accipitur:
Sumit unus, sumunt mille,
Quantum isti, tantum ille,
Nec sumptus consumitur.

8. Whoso eateth it can never
Break the Body, rend or sever;
Christ entire our hearts doth fill:
Thousands eat the bread of heaven,
Yet as much to one is given:
Christ, though eaten, bideth still.

9. Sumunt boni, sumunt mali,
Sorte tamen inaequali
Vitae, vel interitus:
Mors est malis, vita bonis:
Vide, paris sumptionis
Quam sit dispar exitus!

9. Good and bad, they come to greet Him:
Unto life the former eat Him,
And the latter unto death;
These find death and those find heaven;
See, from the same life-seed given,
How the harvest differeth!

10. Fracto demum sacramento
Ne vacilles, sed memento
Tantum esse sub fragmento,
Quantum toto tegitur;
Nulla rei fit scissura,
Signi tantum fit fractura,
Qua nec status, nec statura
Signati minuitur.

10. When at last the bread is broken,
Doubt not what the Lord hath spoken:
In each part the same love-token,
The same Christ, our hearts adore:
For no power the thing divideth—
'Tis the symbols He provideth,
While the Saviour still abideth
Undiminished as before.

11. Ecce, panis angelorum
Factus cibus viatorum,
Vere panis filiorum,
Non mittendus canibus;
In figuris praesignatur,
Cum Isaac immolatur,
Agnus paschae deputatur,
Datur manna patribus.

11. Hail, angelic bread of heaven,
Now the pilgrim's hoping-leaven,
Yea, the bread to children given
That to dogs must not be thrown:
In the figures contemplated,
'Twas with Isaac immolated,
By the Lamb 'twas antedated,
In the manna it was known.

12. Bone pastor, panis vere,
Iesu, nostri miserere,
Tu nos pasce, nos tuere,
Tu nos bona fac videre
In terra viventium.
Tu qui cuncta scis et vales,
Qui nos pascis hic mortales,
Tuos ibi commensales,
Cohaeredes et sodales
Fac sanctorum civium.

12. O Good Shepherd, still confessing
Love, in spite of our transgressing,—
Here Thy blessed food possessing,
Make us share Thine every blessing
In the land of life and love:
Thou, whose power hath all completed
And Thy flesh as food hath meted,
Make us, at Thy table seated,
By Thy saints, as friends be greeted,
In Thy paradise above.

Tr. H. T. Henry (*Eucharistica*, Dolphin Press, Phila., 1912, p. 39-43. Quoted by permission of publishers.)

XVI. *Stabat mater dolorosa*

1. Stabat mater dolorosa Iuxta crucem lacrimosa, Dum pendebat filius, Cuius animam gementem, Contristantem et dolentem Pertransivit gladius.	1. By the Cross her vigil keeping Stands the Queen of sorrows weeping, While her son in torment hangs; Now she feels—O heart afflicted By the sword of old predicted!— More than all a mother's pangs.
2. O quam tristis et afflicta Fuit illa benedicta Mater unigeniti, Quae maerebat et dolebat Et tremebat, dum videbat Nati poenas incyti.	2. Sad and heavy stands beside him She who once had magnified him One—begotten, only—born; While she sees that rich atoning, Long the moaning, deep the groaning Of her mother—heart forlorn.
3. Quis est homo, qui non fleret, Matrem Christi si videret, In tanto supplicio? Quis non posset contristari, Piam matrem contemplari Dolentem cum filio?	3. Who Christ's Mother contemplating In such bitter anguish waiting, Has no human tears to shed? Who would leave Christ's Mother, sharing All the pain her Son is bearing, By those tears uncomforted?
4. Pro peccatis suae gentis Vidit Iesum in tormentis Et flagellis subditum; Vidit suum dulcem natum Morientem, desolatum, Dum emisit spiritum.	4. Victim - priest of Jewry's nation, There he hangs in expiation; Scourge and nail have had their will; Earth and heaven his cause forsaking, Now his noble heart is breaking, Now the labouring breath is still.

5. Eia mater, fons amoris,
Me sentire vim doloris
Fac, ut tecum lugeam;
Fac, ut ardeat cor meum
In amando Christum Deum,
Ut sibi complaceam.

5. Mother, fount whence love flows truest,
Let me know the pain thou knewest,
Let me weep as thou hast wept;
Love divine within me burning,
That diviner love returning,
May thy Son this heart accept.

6. Sancta mater, istud agas,
Crucifixi fige plagas
Corde meo valide;
Tui nati vulnerati,
Tam dignati pro me pati,
Poenas mecum divide.

6. Mother, if my prayer be granted,
Those five wounds of his implanted
In my breast I fain would see;
Love exceeding hangs there bleeding,
My cause pleading, my love needing–
Bid him share his cross with me.

7. Fac me vere tecum flere,
Crucifixo condolere,
Donec ego vixero;
Iuxta crucem tecum stare,
Te libenter sociare
In planctu desidero.

7. Till life fails, I would not fail him,
Still remember, still bewail him,
Born thy Son, and crucified;
By the cross my vigil keeping
I would spend those hours of weeping,
Queen of sorrows, at thy side.

8. Virgo virginum praeclara,
Mihi iam non sis amara,
Fac me tecum plangere;
Fac, ut portem Christi mortem,
Passionis fac consortem
Et plagas recolere.

8. Virgin, boast of all creation,
Heed my tears, nor consolation
In thy bitterness repel;
At thy side his livery wearing,
His cross bearing, his death sharing,
Of these wounds the beads I'll tell.

9. Fac me plagis vulnerari,
Cruce hac inebriari,
Et cruore filii;
Inflammatus et accensus,
Per te, virgo, sim defensus
In die iudicii.

9. Wounds of Christ, in spirit bruise me,
Chalice of his blood, bemuse me,
Cross of Christ, be thou my stay!
Lest I burn in fires unending,
Sinless Maid, my cause befriending,
Shield me at the judgement day!

<table>
<tr><td>10. Fac me cruci custodiri,
Morte Christi praemuniri,

Confoveri gratia.
Quando corpus morietur,
Fac, ut animae donetur
Paradisi gloria.</td><td>10. Jesus, when earth's shadows leave me,
Through thy Mother's prayers receive me
With the palm of victory;
When my body lies forsaken
Let my ransomed soul awaken
Safe, in Paradise, with thee.</td></tr>
</table>

Tr. Ronald A. Knox (*Westminster Hymnal*, Burns, Oates & Washbourne, London, 1940, no. 37. Quoted by permission of publishers.)

XVII. *Salva, festa dies*

(Sarum Processional)

<table>
<tr><td>1. Salve, festa dies, toto venerabilis aevo,
Qua Deus infernum vicit et astra tenet.</td><td>1. Hail thee, Festival Day! blest day that art hallowed forever;
Day wherein Christ arose, breaking the kingdom of death.</td></tr>
<tr><td>2. Ecce, renascentis testatur gratia mundi
omnia cum Domino dona redisse suo.</td><td>2. Lo, the fair beauty of earth, from the death of winter arising,
Every good gift of the year now with its Master returns.</td></tr>
<tr><td>3. Qui crucifixus erat, Deus ecce per omnia regnat,
Dantque creatori cuncta creata precem.</td><td>3. He who was nailed to the cross is God and the ruler of all things;
All things created on earth worship the maker of all.</td></tr>
<tr><td>4. Pollicitam sed redde diem, precor, alma potestas,
Tertia lux rediit; surge, sepulte Deus.</td><td>4. God of all pity and power, let thy word be assured to the doubting;
Light on the third day returns: rise, Son of God, from the tomb!</td></tr>
</table>

5. Non decet ut humili tumulo tua membra tegantur,
Neu pretium mundi vilia saxa premant.

5. Ill doth it seem that thy limbs should linger in lowly dishonor,
Ransom and price of the world, veiled from the vision of men.

6. Indignum est cuius clauduntur cuncta pugillo,
Ut tegat inclusum rupe vetante lapis.

6. Ill it beseemeth that thou by whose hand all things are encompassed,
Captive and bound shouldst remain, deep in the gloom of the rock.

7. Lintea tolle, precor, sudaria linque sepulchro,
Tu satis es nobis, et sine te nihil est.

7. Rise now, O Lord, from the grave and cast off the shroud that enwrapped thee;
Thou art sufficient for us: nothing without thee exists.

8. Funeris exsequias pateris vitae auctor et orbis,
Intras mortis iter dando salutis opem.

8. Mourning they laid thee to rest, who art author of life and creation;
Treading the pathway of death, life thou bestowedst on man.

9. Redde tuam faciem, videant ut saecula lumen,
Redde diem, qui nos te moriente fugit.

9. Show us thy face once more, that the ages may joy in thy brightness;
Give us the light of day, darkened on earth at thy death.

10. Eripis innumerum populum de carcere mortis,
Et sequitur liber, quo suus auctor adit.

10. Out of the prison of death thou art rescuing numberless captives;
Freely they tread in the way whither their maker has gone.

11. Tristia cesserunt infernae vincula legis,
Expavitque chaos luminis ore premi.

11. Jesus has harrowed hell; he has led captivity captive:
Darkness and chaos and death fleé from the face of the light.

Tr. Maurice F. Bell, from *The English Hymnal* by permission of the Oxford University Press.

Notes

Chapter One

Early Middle Ages: Latin Hymns of The Fourth Century

1. Jerome, *Liber de viris illustribus*, 100 (*MPL* 23, 699).

2. *Hilarius autem, Gallus episcopus Pictaviensis, eloquentia conspicuus, hymnorum carmine floruit primus. De ecclesiasticis officiis* 1, 6 (*MPL* 83, 743).

3. W. N. Myers, *The Hymns of Saint Hilary of Poitiers in the Codex Aretinus* (Phila., Un. of Penn., 1928) 12, 29, 53, 67. For a discussion of other hymns attributed to Hilary, see p. 14; also A. S. Walpole, *Early Latin Hymns* (Cambridge, 1922) 1-4. Translations by W. N. Myers.

4. *Antiphonary of Bangor*, edited by F. E. Warren, *Henry Bradshaw Society Publications*, vols. 4, 10 (London, 1893, 1895). For discussion of authorship see vol. 10, 36.

5. Or perhaps Treves.

6. Augustine, *Confessions* 9, 7 (*MPL* 32, 770). Translation from *Confessions of S. Augustine, Ancient and Modern Library of Theol. Literature* (London, 1886).

7. Translations of first lines: W. J. Copeland, C. Bigg, R. E. Messenger, J. M. Neale.

8. Translations of first lines: J. M. Neale, E. Caswall.

9. Translations of first lines: J. M. Neale, H. M. Jones, R. E. Messenger, S. Hurlbut.

10. Myers, *op. cit.* (see note 3) 18-22.

11. G. Reese, *Music in the Middle Ages* (New York, 1940) 104.

12. Caelius Sedulius, 5th C., an early imitator of Ambrose, wrote a well-known alphabetic hymn, *A solis ortus cardine*.

Chapter Two

Early Middle Ages: The Old Hymnal

1. *Regula Sancti Benedicti,* IX.

2. P. Batiffol, *Historie du Breviare romain,* translated by A. M. Y. Bayley (London, 1912), chap. I.

3. Dom A. Wilmart, "Le Psautier de la Reine," *(Cod. Vat. Reg. 11), Revue Benedictine XXVIII* (1911) 376 ff.

4. Walpole, *Early Latin Hymns,* (ch. 1, note 3), xi-xiv.

5. Laodicea, c. 364, Canon 59. See G. D. Mansi, *Sacrorum conciliorum—collectio* (Florence, Venet. et Par., 1763) ii, 573; Braga, 563, Mansi ix, 778.

6. H. F. Muller, "Pre-History of the Medieval Drama," *Zeitschrift f. romanische Philologie* 44 (1924) 544-575.

7. Tours, 567, Mansi xiv, 803.

8. H. Heimbucher, *Die Orden und Kongregationen der katholischen Kirche,* 3 vols. (Paderborn, 1907) vol. I, 224-236, *Ausbreitung der Benediktinerregel.*

9. F. H. Dudden, *Gregory the Great* (London, 1905), 2 vols., II, chap. 8.

10. See *A. H. (Analecta Hymnica Medii Aevi)* 51.24-41, notes. The hymns excepted are nos. 23-30; 34-40; J. Julian, *Dictionary of Hymnology. Gregory I., St., Pope;* C. Blume, "Gregor der Grosse als Hymnendichter," *Stimmen aus Maria-Laach,* 1908, 269 ff.

11. H. LeClercq, *L'Espagne chrétienne* (Paris, 1906) 304-5.

12. Migne, *PL* 80, 642-700, Braulio's Letters.

13. IV Council of Toledo, 633, Canon 2, Mansi x, 616; Canon 13, Mansi x, 622-3. *Sicut igitur orationes, ita et hymnos in laudem Dei compositos, nullus vestrum ulterius improbet, sed pari modo Gallia, Hispaniaque celebret: excommunicatione plectendi, qui hymnos rejicere fuerint ausi.*

14. See R. E. Messenger, "The Mozarabic Hymnal," *TAPhA* 75 (1944) 103-126.

15. *The Irish Liber Hymnorum,* edited by J. H. Bernard and R. Atkinson, *Henry Bradshaw Soc. Pub.* 13, 14 (London, 1897, 1898), 14, 23-6.

16. *Antiphonary of Bangor,* chap. I, note 4; for history of the manuscript now in the Ambrosian Library at Milan, p. xii-xiii.

17. Translations of first lines, 1) J. M. Neale, 2), 3), 4) R. E. Messenger.

18. The Celtic hymns are edited in *A. H.* 51, Part II. See also J. F. Kenney, *Sources for the Early History of Ireland,* 2 vols. (New York, 1929) 252-3, 258-274, *Hymns.*

19. Translations of first lines in Summary by J. M. Neale except 2) C. Bigg, 7) G. R. Woodward.

20. C. W. Douglas, *Church Music in History and Practice* (New York, 1937) 168.

Chapter Three

The Ninth Century Revival: Hymns

1. J. M. Neale and G. H. Forbes, *The Ancient Liturgies of the Gallican Church* (Burntisland, 1855) p. v.

2. P. Jaffé, *Regesta Pontificum Romanorum* (Lipsiae, 1885-8) 2473 (1900).

3. *Monumenta Germaniae Historica, Legum sectio,* II, *Capitularia Regum Francorum,* I, *Capitulare primum,* 769; *Capitulare Haristallense,* 779; *Admonitio generalis,* 789; *Synodus Franconofurtensis,* 794; *Epistola de litteris colendis,* 780-800; *Epistola generalis,* 786-800; *Capitulare missorum generale,* 802; *Capitularia missorum specialia,* 802; *Synodus et conventus aquisgrani habita,* 802; *Capitulare de examinandis ecclesiasticis,* 802; *Capitulare missorum,* 803; *Capitulare de causis etc.,* 811; *Capitulare aquisgranense,* 801-813; *Capitulare cum episcopis etc.,* 780-790; *Capitulare mantuanum primum,* no date, p. 194; *Pippini capitulare Italicum,* 801-810.

4. *MGH, Legum sectio,* II, *Capitularia Regum Francorum,* I, *Epistola generalis,* no. 30, p. 80; P. Jaffé, *Bibliotheca Rerum Germanicarum,* vol. IV, *Monumenta Carolina* (Berlin, 1867) 139, 140.

5. Dom R. Van Doren, *Étude sur l'influence musicale de l'abbaye de Saint-Gall* (Louvain, 1925) ch. vi, Metz.

6. E. Mühlbacher, *Deutsche Geschichte unter den Karolingern* (Stuttgart, 1896) 211; Jaffé, *Monumenta Carolina,* 358ff.

7. E. Bishop, *Liturgica Historica* (Oxford, 1918) 49-55.

8. A. Fortescue, *The Mass* (London, 1914) 183.

9. In *Monumenta Germaniae Historica—Poetarum latinorum medii aevi,* vol. iv, edited by P. von Winterfeld (Berlin, 1923).

10. W. Turner, "Irish Teachers in the Carolingian Revival of Learning," *Cath. Un. Bulletin,* XIII (Washington, 1907) 384-5; J. J. O'Kelly, *Ireland: Elements of her Early Story* (Dublin, 1921) ch. viii, *Early Irish on the Continent.*

11. Einhard, *Vita Caroli,* 21.

12. L. Gougaud, *Gaelic Pioneers of Christianity, VI-XII Century* (Dublin, 1923) 60-3. Translated by Victor Collins.

13. S. Singer, *Die Dichterschule von St. Gallen* (Leipzig, 1922) *Introd.* (by Peter Wagner) 11.

14. Turner, *supra,* 570; J. M. Clark, *The Abbey of St. Gall as a Center of Literature and Art* (Cambridge, 1926) 31.

15. *Annales Laurissenses, anno* 757 (*MGH, SS,* I, 140).

16. Jaffé, *Regesta,* 2346 (1799); Notker Balbulus, *Epistolae* (*MPL,* 131, 1172); *Gesta Caroli,* II, 7.

17. F. H. Dudden, *Gregory the Great* (ch. 2, note 9) I, ch. *VI Gregory at Constantinople.*

18. P. Wagner, "Morgen-und Abendland in der Musikgeschichte," *Stimmen der Zeit,* Bd. 114 (1927) 138.

19. Clark, *The Abbey of St. Gall etc.,* 112; C. Diehl, *Manuel d'Art Byzantin* (Paris, 1910) 359-360, 362-3; M. Hauttmann, *Die Kunst des frühen Mittelalters* (Berlin, 1929) 51-62; J. Strzygowski, *Origin of Christian Church Art* (Oxford, 1923) 84.

20. *Anal. Hymn.,* 51, *Introduction,* xvii-xix; extended lists of the later Latin hymns appear in J. Julian, *Dictionary of Hymnology* (London, 1925) 546, 547.

21. J. Mearns, *Early Latin Hymnaries* (Cambridge, 1913).

22. Walpole, *Early Latin Hymns,* (ch. 1, note 3) xi.

23. Walpole, *ibid,* xii; W. H. Frere, Introduction to *Hymns Ancient and Modern Historical Edition* (London, 1909); Wilmart, *Le Psautier de la Reine etc.,* 362-3; F. J. E. Raby, *Christian Latin Poetry* (Oxford, 1927) 38-41. See also R. E. Messenger, "Whence the Ninth Century Hymnal?," *TAPhA* 69 (1938) 446-464.

24. Gesta Caroli, I, 10; Einhard, *Vita Caroli,* edited by Garrod and Mowat (Oxford, 1915), Appendix, p. xxxvii.

25. Heimbucher, *Die Orden und Congregationen* etc., vol. I, 235, 237-9; *Jahrbücher der deutschen Geschichte* (Berlin & Leipzig, 1866-1902), *Geschichte des Ostfrankischen Reichs,* vol. II, 39, 42, 46.

26. Alcuin, *De psalmorum usu* (*MPL,* 101), *Officia per ferias MPL,* 101, *Epistolae* 84, 94, 164, 227 (*MPL,* 101): Rabanus Maurus, *De clericis institutés,* II, 49 (*MPL,* 107, 362): Amalarius of Metz, *De officiis divinis* (continuation) in J. Mabillon, *Vetera Analecta* (Paris, 1723) 99; Walafrid Strabo, *De ecclesiasticarum rerum exordiis* etc., ch. xxv (*MPL,* 114, 952ff.).

27. H. De Boor, *Die deutsche Literatur* 770-1170 (München, 1949) 21.

28. P. Batiffol, *History of the Roman Breviary* (London, 1912) 143-4.

29. *Anal. Hymn.* 51.

30. Translation of first line, J. M. Neale.

31. Dom P. B. Gams, *Die Kirchengeschichte von Spanien* (Regensburg, 1862-1879) II, Pt. 2, 302, 326-9; Z. Garcia Villada, *Historia eclesiástica de España* (Madrid, 1929-36) V, 85.

32. De Urbel, "Los himnos mozárabes," *Revista ecles. Silos* 58 (1927) 56-61.

33. E. Bishop, "Spanish Symptoms," *Liturgica Historica* (Oxford, 1918) 168.

34. L. Wiener, *Contributions toward a History of Arabico-Gothic Culture* (New York, 1917-21) 101; H. G. Farmer, *Historical Facts for the Arabian Musical Influence* (London, 1930) 23.

35. *Anal. Hymn.* 51, *Introduction.*

Chapter Four

The Ninth Century Revival: Sequences

1. Fortescue, *The Mass* (See ch. 3, note 8) 268-9.

2. See *Introduction* to *A. H.* 53, by C. Blume and H. M. Bannister. This *Introduction* has been used as the basis for the discussion of sequence origins. Theories and opinions of others are noted from time to time.

3. W. H. Frere, Introduction to *Hymns Ancient and Modern* (See ch. 3, note 23) xxviii; P. Wagner, *Introduction to Gregorian Melodies* (London, 1907) 223, translation by Orme and Wyatt.

4. G. Reese, *Music in the Middle Ages* (ch. I, note 11) *passim*. This book contains an excellent standard account of the musical aspect of the sequence.

5. G. Schnürer, *Kirche und Kultur im Abendland* (Paderborn, 1926) II, 88.

6. W. Christ, "Über die Bedeutung von Hirmos, etc.," *Sitzungberichte der kön. bay. Akad. der Wissenschaft zu München*, II (1870) 89f.

7. A. Gastoué, "Les Types byzantins de la Sequence," *Tribune de Saint-Gervais*, Dec. 1922, 1, 2.

8. Frere, *Introduction, supra,* xxiv.

9. L. Gautier, *Histoire de la poésie liturgique au Moyen âge* (Paris, 1886) 1.

10. A. Gastoué, "Les Origines liturgiques de la séquence," *Tribune de Saint-Gervais*, June, 1922. See also Wetzer and Welte, *Kirchenlexicon, Sequenzen:* an important article.

11. Amalarius, *De ecclesiasticis officiis,* III, 16 (*MPL,* 105, 1123).

12. J. Ottenwälder, "Griechisch-byzantinische Einflüsse," *Theol. Quartalschr.* XCVII (1915), 564-7.

13. Reese, *Music in the Middle Ages, supra,* 133.

14. S. Singer, *Die Dichterschule von St. Gallen* (ch. 3, note 13), *Introduction,* 14, 15.

15. The earliest manuscript is *Antiphonale missarum S. Gregorii,* codex 239 of Laon; see *Paléographie musicale,* X. A. Gastoué, *Les Origines du Chant Romain* (Paris, 1907) 250f.

16. Wetzer und Welte, *supra, Sequenzen.*

17. Frere, *Introduction, supra,* xxviii-xxix; Notker Balbulus, *Liber sequentiarum, Praefatio* (*MPL,* 131, 1003).

18. P. Wagner, "Morgen und Abendland in der Musikgeschichte," (ch. 3, note 18) 139; Schnürer, *supra,* II, 88.

19. Gastoué, "Les Types byzantins de la Séquence," *supra,* 2.

20. W. Meyer, *Gesammelte Abhandlungen zur mittellateinischen Rythmik* (Berlin, 1908) 37.

21. P. Von Winterfeld, *Stilfragen aus der lateinischen Dichtung des Mittelalters* in *Deutsche Dichter etc.* (München, 1922) 442.

22. W. Meyer, *supra,* 41: "So ist die lyrische Dichtung des Mittelalters durchaus dem Kirchengesang neu geboren worden."

23. E. Wellesz, *Eastern Elements in Western Chant. Studies in the Early History of Ecclesiastical Music* (Oxford, 1947) Pt. IV, ch. 1, *Origin of sequences and tropes,* an excellent summary of the subject as investigated to 1947.

24. Notker, *supra,* note 17.

25. P. A. Schubiger, *Die Sängerschule St. Gallens vom viii.-xii. Jahrhundert* (Einsiedeln, 1858); W. Wilmanns, "Welche Sequenzen hat Notker verfasst?," *Zeitschrift f. deutsches Altertum,* XV (1872) 267f.; J. Werner, *Notkers Sequenzen. Beiträge zur Geschichte der Lat. Sequenzendichtung* (Aarau, 1901) III, IV; S. Singer, *supra;* Van Doren, (ch. 3, note 5) ch. 9; Clark, (ch. 3, note 14) 175. W. von den Steinen, *Notker der Dichter und seine geistliche Welt,* 2 vols. (Bern. 1948). This author reviews previous literature.

26. Ottenwälder, *supra,* 464-5.

27. They are *Canopica, Styx, Phlegethon, sophia, herous, Myrmidonas, spermologos.*

28. P. S. Allen, *Romanesque Lyric* (Un. of North Carolina Press, 1928) 66, 221, 222; Schnürer, *supra,* 89; Wellesz. *supra,* 165; W. B. Sedgwick, "Origin of Rhyme," "*Revue Bénédictine* XXXVI (1924), 341.

29. Several attractive illustrations of the *modus* may be found in Karl Breul's edition of *The Cambridge Songs* (Cambridge, 1915).

30. Schnürer, *supra,* 89; R. Molitor, *Die Musik in der Reichnau,* reviewed in *Jahrbuch f. Liturgiewissenschaft* VI (1926) 331.

31. See Chapter VII.

Chapter Five

Late Middle Ages: Hymns and Sequences

1. J. De Ghellinck, S. J., *L'Essor de la Littérature Latine au XIIe Siècle*, 2 vols. (Brussels, 1946) II, 285.

2. M. Hélin, *History of Medieval Latin Literature* (New York, 1949), translated by J. C. Snow from *Littérature d'occident: Histoire des Lettres latines du Moyen Age*, 79.

3. L. Gautier, *Oeuvres poétiques d'Adam de Saint-Victor*, 2 vols. (Paris, 1858-9); E. Misset et P. Aubry, *Les Proses d'Adam de Saint-Victor* (Paris, 1900).

4. Translations of first lines: R. Messenger, Anon, E. Caswall.

5. Translations of first lines: S. A. Hurlbut, R. Messenger.

6. *A. H.* 48. 141-232.

7. Translations of first lines: 1 and 2, H. Waddell; 3 and 5, E. Caswall; 4, R. Messenger.

8. Hélin, *supra*, 117.

9. P. Wagner, *Introduction to the Gregorian Melodies* (ch. 4, note 3) 241.

10. Translations of first lines: 1 and 4, R. A. Knox; 2, H. T. Henry; 3, W. J. Irons.

11. Translation of first line: R. Messenger.

12. R. E. Messenger, "Hymns and Sequences of the Sarum Use," *TAPhA*, 59 (1928) 99-129.

13. E. Bishop, *Liturgica Historica* (Oxford, 1918) 211-37.

14. E. Hoskins, *Horae Beatae Mariae Virginis etc.* (London, 1901); H. Bohatta, *Bibliographie des livres d'heures* (Wien, 1924), 2nd edition.

15. R. E. Messenger, "Hymns in the Horae Eboracenses," *Classical Weekly*, 38 (Jan., 1945) 90-5.

16. S. Singer, "Arabische und europäische Poesie im Mittelalter, *Zeitschrift f. deutsche Philologie*, LII (April, 1927); K. Burdach, "Über den Ursprung des mittelalterichen Minnesangs, etc." in *Vorspiel* I (Halle, 1925) 311; A. F. Von Schack, *Poesie und Kunst der Araber etc.*, 2 vols. (Stuttgart, 1877) II, 101-5.

17. C. F. Brown, *Religious Lyrics of the 14th Century* (Oxford, 1924). Translations of William Herebert (d. 1333) xiii.

18. *Ad honorem Regis summi*, translation of first line: R. E. Messenger. See C. Daux, *Les Chansons des Pèlerins de St. Jacques* (Montauban, 1899).

19. A. S. Walpole, *Early Latin Hymns*, (ch. 1, note 3) 87-92.

20. E. Rodgers, *Discussion of Holidays in the Later Middle Ages* (New York

1940) 33. Miss Rodgers sums up the evidence here, reaching an affirmative conclusion.

21. L. Thorndike, "Elementary and Secondary Education in the Middle Ages," *Speculum*, 15 (1940) 400-8, p. 401.

22. W. O. Wehrle, *Macaronic Hymn Tradition etc.* (Washington, 1933).

Chapter Six

Late Middle Ages: Processional Hymns

1. *Matt.* 21: 4-11; *Mark* 11: 7-11; *Luke* 19: 35-38; *John* 12: 12-5.

2. Basil, *Ep.* 207, *Ad Neocaes, MPG* 32. 765; Ambrose, *Ep.* 40. 16, *Ad Theodosium, MPL* 16. 1107; Sozomen, *Hist. Eccles.* VIII, 8; see also Tertullian, *Ad uxorem*, II, 4, *MPL* 1. 1294.

3. *St. Silviae, quae fertur, Peregrinatio ad loca sancta*, in *Itinera Hiersolymitana, Saeculi III-VIII*, ed. P. Geyer (Vindobonae, 1898) *CSEL* 39. 35-101.

4. *Ibid.* XXIV, 1-7, 8-12; XXV, 7; XXVI; XXXI; XL, 1-2.

5. A. Bludau, *Die Pilgerreise der Aetheria, Studien zur Gesch. u. Kultur d. Altertums XV*, 1/2, (Paderborn, 1927) 56. Translation, Robert Bridges.

6. A. Baumstark, *Die Idiomela der byzantinischen Karfreitshoren etc.* Reviewed in *Jahrbuch f. Liturgiewissenschaft*, 10 (1930) 339-40.

7. P. Batiffol, *Études de liturgie et d'archéologie chrétienne*, (Paris, 1919) ch. VI, *La Chandeleur*, p. 200.

8. Ambrose, *Ep.* 11(53), *MPL* 17. 743-4; Augustine, *De Civ. Dei* 22. 8; *Conf.* 9. 7; See also the hymn *Grates tibi, Jesu, novas*, attributed to Ambrose, *A. H.* 50. 17.

9. G. H. Cobb, "Early Catholic Outdoor Processions," *The Month*, 148 (1926) 539-542.

10. For Mamertus, see Greg. Turonen., *Hist. franc.* 2. 34, *MPL* 71. 230-32. *Councils.* Council of Orleans, 511, canon 17, Mansi VIII, 355; Council of Girona, 517, *Capit.* 2 & 3, Mansi, VIII, 549; see also 17th Council of Toledo, 694, *Capit.* 6, Mansi XII, 99-100. *Litaniae maiores*, Greg. Magnus, *Ep.* V, 11, Litany on Feast of St. John Baptist, *MPL* 77, 732-3; *Litania septiformis*, Greg. Turonen., *Hist. franc.* 10, 1, *MPL* 71. 519-20; Joh. Diac., *Vita Greg. Magn.*, 1. 41, 42, MPL 75. 80.

11. L. Duchesne, *Christian Worship*, (London, 1904) 240, 515.

12. P. Batiffol, (note 7) 197-201; L. Eisenhofer, *Handbuch der Katholischen Liturgik*, 2 vols. (Freiburg in Breisgau, 1923) I, 582-6.

13. At this point the definition of *processio* in Canon Law is of interest: *Nomine sacrarum processionum significantur solemnes supplicationes quae a populi fideli, duce*

clero, fiunt eundo ordinatim de loco sacro ad locum sacrum, ad excitandam fidelium pietatem, ad commemoranda Dei beneficia eique gratias agendas, ad divinum auxilium implorandum. Can. 1290. ç 1.

14. B. M. Peebles, "Fortunatus, Poet of the Holy Cross," *Amer. Church Monthly* 38 (1935, July-Sept.) 152-166. His account is based upon Greg. Turonen., *Hist. franc.*, IX, 40; Baudonovia, *Vita S. Rad.*, II. 16.

15. R. E. Messenger, *Salve festa dies, TAPhA*, 78 (1947) 208-222. Translation, S. A. Hurlbut; for *Salve festa dies,* traditional.

16. Dom M. Férotin, *Liber ordinum*, in *Monumenta ecclesiae liturgica*, 5 (Paris, 1904) 178-87; Isidore of Seville, *De ecclesiasticis officiis*, 1. 38.

17. Férotin, *supra*, 179.

18. A. S. Walpole, *Early Latin Hymns*, (ch. 1, note 3) 337-340. Translation, 1st line, Walpole.

19. Duchesne, *supra*, 162-4.

20. Walpole, *supra*, 342-4.

21. Translations in this chapter, unless otherwise noted, are furnished by the author.

22. L. Gautier, *Histoire de la Poésie liturgique etc.* (ch. 4, note 9) ch. VI, *Versus.*

23. Von den Steinen, *Notker der Dichter etc.* (ch. 4, note 25) I, 40-42.

24. Eisenhofer (see note 12) I, 522-3.

25. Dom A. Wilmart, *Auteurs spirituels etc.* (Paris, 1932) 26-36.

26. R. E. Messenger, *Sancta Maria quid est?, Cath. Choirmaster*, June, 1950.

27. Eisenhofer, *supra*, I, 100-102.

28. Du Cange, see *versarius.*

29. Gulielmus Durandus, *Rationale divinorum officiorum* (Lugdini, 1612) Bk. IV, *De accessu sacerdotis ac pontificis ad altare et de Processione.*

30. *Ibid.* fol. 102.

31. D. Attwater, *Dictionary of Saints* (London, 1938) 180.

32. G. Reese, *Music in the Middle Ages* (ch. 1, note 11) 201.

33. L. Ellinwood, "The Conductus," *Musical Quarterly*, 27 (1941) 2. 165-203.

Chapter Seven

Influence and Survival of Latin Hymns

1. W. B. Sedgwick, "The Origin of Rhyme," (ch. 4, note 28) 333.

2. For translations see Helen J. Waddell, *Medieval Latin Lyrics* (London, 1929); *The Wandering Scholars* (New York, 1949), new edition.

3. P. S. Allen, *Romanesque Lyric* (ch. 4, note 28), Ch. XII, especially p. 223.

4. F. J. E. Raby, *History of Secular Latin poetry in the Middle Ages*, 2 vols. (Oxford, 1934) II, 332.

5. E. M. Sanford, "Were the Hymns of Prudentius actually sung?" *Classical Philology* 31 (1936) 71.

6. For the texts of liturgical plays, see K. Young, "*The Drama of the Medieval Church*, 2 vols. (Oxford, 1933).

7. B. M. Peebles, "O Roma nobilis," *Amer. Benedictine Review*, I (1950) no. 1.

8. R. Stroppel, *Liturgie und geistliche Dichtung* (Frankfort am Main, 1927) 53-5: S. Singer, "Karolingische Renaissance," *Germanisch-Romanisch Monatschrift*, 13 (1925) 200-1.

9. K. E. Wackernagel, *Das deutsche Kirchenlied etc.*, 5 vols. (Leipzig, 1864-77) vol. I.

10. K. Meyer, *Selections from Ancient Irish Poetry* (London, 1911) *Introd.* 13.

11. J. Pokorny, *Die älteste Lyrik der grünen Insel* (Halle S., 1923) 13, 14.

12. W. Meyer, "Liturgie, Kunst und Dichtung in Mittelalter," *Gesammelte Abhandlungen* (Berlin, 1905) 371.

13. P. von Winterfeld, "Stilfragen der lateinischen Dichtung des Mittelalters," *Deutsche Dichter des lateinischen Mittelalters* (München, 1922) 440.

14. Washington, D. C., Catholic Un. Press, 1942, especially p. 221, 231, 248, 266.

15. H. Koht, "Medieval Liberty Poems," *Amer. Hist. Review*, 48 (1943) no. 2, 281-290.

16. H. Spanke, "Über das Fortleben der Sequenzenform in den Romanischen Sprachens," *Zeitschrift f. Rom. Philol.* 51 (1931) 309-334.

17. E. A. Peers. *Ramon Lull* (London, 1929) 140.

18. See translation by H. C. Robbins, 1939, "Most High, Omnipotent, Good Lord."

19. For a brief account, see J. Pulver, "Laudi spirituali," *Musical Opinion*, March, 1938, 503-4; April, 1938, 602-3; May, 1938, 691-2.

20. See Bibliography for these titles.

21. Dom Jean Stéphan, *The Adeste fideles*, "Publications," Buckfast Abbey, South Devon, England, 1947. Translation, Frederick Oakeley.

22. M. Britt, *Hymns of the Breviary and Missal* (New York, 1922, 1948), a standard and indispensable work.

Bibliography

I. Bibliographies

Leclercq, L., Article "Hymnes". *Dictionnaire d'archéologie chrétienne et de liturgie.* Contains extensive bibliography upon the subject of medieval hymnology.

Farrar, C. P. and Evans, A. P., *Bibliography of English Translations from medieval sources.* New York, 1946. Hymns, 2025-2045.

Raby, F. J. E., *History of Christian-Latin poetry from the beginning to the close of the Middle Ages.* Oxford, 1927. Bibliography classified by authors and periods.

Reese, G., *Music in the Middle Ages.* New York, 1941. Contains extensive bibliography including many periodical articles.

II. Collections and Indices

Analecta hymnica medii aevi, edited by C. Blume and G. M. Dreves, 55 vols. Leipzig, 1886-1922. Introductions most informative.

Analecta liturgica, part 2, vols. I, *Thesaurus hymnologicus;* II, *Prosae,* edited by E. Misset and W. H. J. Weale. Insulis et Brugis, 1888-1902.

Blume, C. and Dreves, G. M., *Hymnologische Beiträge* (Quellen und Forschungen zur Geschichte der lateinischen Hymnendichtungen, 2 vols.). Leipzig, 1897-1901.

Chevalier, C. U. J., *Repertorium hymnologicum,* catalogue des chants, hymnes, proses, sequences, tropes, 6 vols. Louvain, Bruxelles, 1892-1920. Published as supplements to the *Analecta Bollandiana.*

Daniel, H. A., *Thesaurus hymnologicus,* 5 vols. Lipsiae, 1855-1856, 2nd edition.

Gaselee, S., *The Oxford Book of medieval Latin verse.* Oxford, 1928.

Germing, M., *Latin hymns.* Chicago, 1920. Text book.

del Grande, C., *Liturgiae preces hymni Christianorum e papyris collecti.* Neapel, 1934.

Grenfell, B. and Hunt, A., *Oxyrhynchus papyri, Part XV*. London, 1922.

Harris, R. and Mingana, A., *The odes and psalms of Solomon, I. Text, II. Translation*. Manchester, 1916-1920.

Hurlbut, S. A., *Hortus conclusus, Medieval Latin hymns with English renderings*, 10 parts. Washington, D. C., 1930-1936.

Kehrein, J., *Lateinische Sequenzen des Mittelalters*. Mainz, 1873. The most extensive collection of sequences made up to that date.

Mc Dougall, A. G., *Pange lingua: breviary hymns of old uses with an English rendering*. London, 1916.

Mearns, J., *Canticles of the Christian Church eastern and western in early and medieval times*. Cambridge, 1914.

Merrill, W. A., *Latin hymns*. New York, 1917. Text book.

Mone, F. J., *Lateinische Hymnen des Mittelalters*, 3 vols. Freiburg im Breisgau, 1853-1855.

Morel, G., *Lateinische Hymnen des Mittelalters*, grosstentheils aus Handschriften schweizerischen Kloster, als Nachtrag zu den Hymnensammlungen von Mone, Daniel & Andern. Einsiedeln, 1866.

Neale, J. M., *Hymni ecclesiae e breviariis quibusdam et missalibus Gallicanis, Germanis, Hispanis, Lusitanis desumpti*. Oxford, 1851.

———, *Sequentiae ex missalibus Germanis, Anglicis, Gallicis, aliisque medii aevi, collectae*. London, 1852.

Newman, J. H., *Hymni ecclesiae,* London, 1838, 1865.

Phillimore, J. S., *The hundred best Latin hymns*. London, 1926. Attractive anthology.

Poetae latini aevi Carolini in *Monumenta Germaniae Historica . . . Poetarum latinorum medii aevi*, vol. iv, edited by P. von Winterfeld. Berlin, 1923.

Roth, F. W. E., *Lateinische Hymnen des Mittelalters*. Augsburg, 1887. Intended as a supplement to larger collections.

Wackernagel, K. E., *Das deutschen Kirchenlied*, 5 vols. Leipzig, 1864-1877. Vol. I contains Latin hymns.

Walpole, A. S., *Early Latin hymns*. Cambridge, 1922.

Weale, W. H. J., *Analecta liturgica*, Part II, vols. I, II, *Thesaurus hymnologicus - Prosae*. Insulis et Brugis, 1888-1902.

III. History and Authors of Latin Hymns

Allen, P. S., *Mediaeval Latin lyrics*. Chicago, 1931.

Baldwin, C. S., *Medieval rhetoric and poetic*. New York, 1928.

Bardenhewer, O., *Geschichte der altkirchlichen Literatur*, 5 vols. Freiburg in Breisgau, 1912-1932.

Beck, C., *Mittellateinische Dichtung*. Berlin, 1927.

Benson, L. F., *Hymnody of the Christian church*. New York, 1927.

Biraghi, L., *Inni sinceri e carmi di Sant'Ambrogio*. Milano, 1862.

Blume, C., Articles "Hymn", "Hymnody and Hymnology." *Cath. Enc.*

Coulter, C. C., "Latin hymns of the Middle Ages", *Studies in Philology*, 21 (1924) 571-585.

DeGhellinck, J., S. J., *Littérature Latine au Moyen Age*, 2 vols. Paris, 1939.

———, *Littérature Latine au XIIe Siecle*, 2 vols. Brussels, 1946.

De Labriolle, P., *Histoire de la Littérature latine chrétienne*. Paris, 1924. Translation by H. Wilson, *History and Literature of Christianity from Tertullian to Boethius*. New York, 1925.

Donahue, D. J., "The sacred songs of the Middle Ages", *Cath. Hist. Rev.*, *N. S.* vol. 3 (1923) 217-235.

Dreves, G. M., *Ein Jahrtausend lateinischer Hymnendichtung*, Eine Blütenlese aus den Anal. hymn. mit literarhistorischen Erläuterungen, 2 vols. Leipzig, 1909.

Duckett, E. S., *Gateway to the Middle Ages*. New York, 1938.

———, *Latin writers of the 5th century*. New York, 1930.

Dudden, F. H., *Gregory the Great. His place in history and thought*, 2 vols. New York, 1905.

———, *The life and times of St. Ambrose*, 2 vols. Oxford, 1935.

Duffield, S. W., *The Latin hymn-writers and their hymns*. New York, 1889.

Ebert, A., *Allgemeine Geschichte der Literatur des Mittelalters im Abendlande*, 3 vols. Leipzig, 1880-1889. 2nd edition of vol. I.

Gastoué, A., "Proses et séquences", *Tribune d. S. Gervais* (1922), 69-72; "Les origines liturgiques latines de la séquence", 153-158; "Les types byzantins de la séquence", (1923) 1-6.

Gautier, L., *Oeuvres poétiques d'Adam de Saint-Victor*. Paris, 1881.

Gillman, F. J., *Evolution of the English hymn*. New York, 1927.

Heider, A. B., *The Blessed Virgin in early Christian Latin poetry*. Washington, D. C., 1918.

Hélin, M., *History of medieval Latin literature*. New York, 1949. Translated by J. C. Snow from *Littérature d'occident: Histoire des lettres Latines du Moyen Age*.

Hughes, H. V., Dom Anselm, *Latin Hymnody*. London, 1922.

Julian, J., *Dictionary of hymnology*. London, 1925.

Kayser, J., *Breiträge zur Geschichte und Erklärung der ältesten Kirchenhymnen*, 2 vols. Paderborn, 1881, 1886.

Koebner, R., *Venantius Fortunatus*. Leipzig, 1915.

Kroll, J., *Die christliche Hymnodik bis zu Klemens von Alexandreia*. Königsburg: Prog. d. Ak. von Braunsberg, 1921-2. s. 47-98.

———, "Die Hymnendichtung des frühen Christentums", *Die Antike*, 2 (1926) 258-281.

Kuhnmuench, O., S. J., *Early Christian Latin poets from the 4th-6th century*. Chicago, 1929.

Lynch, C. H., *St. Braulio, Bishop of Saragossa*. Washington, D. C., 1938.

Mac Gilton, A. K., *Study of Latin hymns*. Boston, 1918.

Manitius, M., *Geschichte der christlich-lateinischen Poesie bis zur Mitte des 8. Jahrhunderts*. Stuttgart, 1891.

———, *Geschichte der lateinischen Literatur des Mittelalters*, 3 vols. München, 1911-1931.

Maryosip, M., *The oldest Christian hymn-book*. Temple, Texas, 1948.

Meyer, W., *Der Gelegenheitsdichter Venantius Fortunatus*. Berlin, 1901.

Misset, E. et Aubry, P., *Les Proses d'Adam de Saint-Victor*, texte et musique. Paris, 1900.

Myers, W. N., *The hymns of Saint Hilary of Poitiers in the codex Aretinus*. Phila., 1928.

Peebles, B. M., "Fortunatus, poet of the Holy Cross", *Amer. Church Monthly*, 38 (1935) 152-166.

———, *The Poet Prudentius*. Boston College Candlemas Lectures on Christian Literature: no. 2. New York, 1951.

Phillips, C. S., *Hymnody past and present*. London, 1937.

Rand, E. K., *Founders of the Middle Ages*. Cambridge, 1928.

Sage, C. M., *Paul Albar of Cordova: Studies on his life and writings*. Washington, D. C., 1943.

Tardi, D., *Fortunat. Étude sur un dernier représentant de la poésie latine le Gaule merovingienne*. Paris, 1927.

Trench, R. C., *Sacred Latin poetry*. London, 1874.

Weyman, C., *Beiträge zur Geschichte der christlich-lateinischen Poesie*. München, 1926.

Wilmart, A. Dom, *Auteurs spirituels et textes dévots du moyen âge Latin. Études d'histoire litteraire.* Paris, 1932.

———, "Le Psautier de la reine, N. XI, sa provenance et sa date", *Revue Bénédictine,* July-Oct. 1911, 341 ff.

Wrangham, D. S., *Liturgical poetry of Adam of St. Victor.* London, 1881.

IV. Hymns and Liturgy

Antiphonarium Hartkeri, saec. XI, St. Gall MS, 390-391, p. 15-16. *Paléographie Musicale,* Deuxième Série, Tome 1.

Antiphonary of Bangor, An early Irish manuscript in the Ambrosian Library at Milan, edited by F. E. Warren. Henry Bradshaw Society Pub. vols. 4, 10. London, 1893, 1895.

Batiffol, P., *Études de liturgie et d'archèologie chrétienne,* Ch. VI, *La Chandeleur,* 193-215. Paris, 1919.

———, *History of the Roman Breviary.* Translated from the 3rd French edition by A. M. Baylay. London, 1912.

Bishop, E., *Liturgica historica,* Oxford, 1918.

———, "Spanish Symptoms", *Theological Studies,* 8 (1907) 278-294.

———, *The Mozarabic and Ambrosian Rites.* London, 1924.

Blume, C., *Der cursus S. Benedicti Nursini und die liturgischen Hymnen des 6. - 9. Jahrhunderts.* Leipzig, 1908.

———, *Unsere liturgischen Lieder.* Regensburg, 1932.

Bohatta, H., *Bibliographie der livres d'heures* etc. Wien, 1924, 2nd ed.

Breviarium Gothicum, edited by A. Lorenzana. Madrid, 1775. See Migne, *P. L.,* 86.

Britt, M., *Hymns of the Breviary and Missal.* New York, 1922, 1948.

Buchanan, E. S., *An early Latin song-book.* New York, 1930. 13th C. Ms.

Burgess, H., *Select metrical hymns and homilies of Ephrem Syrus.* London, 1855.

Chambers, J. D., *Divine worship in England* in the 13th and 14th, contrasted with and adapted to that in the 19th C. London, 1877.

Chatfield, A. W., *Songs and hymns of the earliest Greek Christian poets.* London, 1876.

Dowden, J., *Church year and kalendar.* Cambridge, 1910.

Duchesne, L., *Origines du culte chrétien.* Translation *Christian worship: origin and evolution* from the 3rd French edition by M. L. McClure. London, 1904.

Durandus, Gulielmus, *Rationale divinorum officiorum* (1286). Lugduni, 1612.

Fisher, A. H., *Cathedral church of Hereford.* London, 1898.

Fortescue, A., *Concerning Hymns.* See Introduction to A. G. McDougall, *Pange lingua,* above.

———, *The Mass: a study of the Roman liturgy.* London, 1914.

Gautier, L., *Histoire de la Poésie liturgique au Moyen Age. Les Tropes.* Paris, 1886.

Hereford Breviary, edited by W. H. Frere and L. E. G. Brown. Henry Bradshaw Society Pub. vols. 26, 40. London, 1904, 1911.

Horae Beatae Mariae Virginis or Sarum and York Primers, edited by E. Hoskins. London, 1901.

Horae Eboracenses, Prymer or Hours of the B. V. M., edited by C. Wordsworth. Surtees Society Pub. vol. 132. London, 1919.

Hymnale secundum usum . . . ecclesiae Sarisburiensis, edited by A. C. Wilson and Dr. Stubbs. Littlemore, 1850.

Hymnarium Sarisburiense. London, 1851. Incomplete.

The Hymner, Translations of the hymns from the Sarum Breviary together with sundry sequences and processions. London, 1905.

Hymns, Ancient and Modern, historical edition. London, 1909. Introduction by W. H. Frere on history of hymns, treats Latin hymns from liturgical point of view.

Irish Liber Hymnorum, edited by J. H. Bernard and R. Atkinson. Henry Bradshaw Society Pub. vols. 13, 14. London, 1897, 1898.

Jahrbuch für Liturgiewissenschaft, edited by O. Casel, O. S. B. Münster i. W., 1921-1934. Vol. xiv (1934) was published in 1938. Invaluable bibliography for every field of medieval hymnology. Many reviews of articles otherwise unobtainable.

Jones, W. H., *Diocesan histories: Salisbury.* London, 1880.

Latin hymns of the Anglo-Saxon church, edited by J. Stevenson. Surtees Society Pub. vol. 23. Durham, 1851.

McClure, M. L. and Feltoe, E. L., *The Pilgrimage of Etheria.* Translations of Christian literature, Series III, Liturgical texts. London, 1919.

Manuale et processionale ad usum insignis ecclesiae Eboracensis, edited by W. G. Henderson. Surtees Society Pub. vol. 63. Durham, 1875.

Maskell, W., *Ancient liturgy of the church of England.* Oxford, 1882. 3rd edition.

———, *Monumenta ritualia ecclesiae Anglicanae,* 3 vols. Oxford, 1882. 2nd edition.

Mearns, J., *Early Latin hymnaries,* an index of hymns in hymnaries before 1100, with an appendix from later sources. Cambridge, 1913.

Missale ad usum insignis ecclesiae Eboracensis, edited by W. G. Henderson. Surtees Society Pub. vols. 59, 60. Durham, 1874.

Missale ad usum percelebris ecclesiae Herfordensis, edited by W. G. Henderson. Leeds, 1874.

Missale mixtum, edited by A. Lesley, S. J. Rome, 1755. See Migne, *P. L.* 86.

Mozarabic Psalter, edited by J. P. Gilson. Henry Bradshaw Society Pub. vol. 30. London, 1905.

Neale, J. M. and Forbes, G. H., *The ancient liturgies of the Gallican church.* Burntisland, 1855.

Ordinale and customary of the Benedictine nuns of Barking abbey, edited by J. B. L. Tolhurst. Henry Bradshaw Society Pub. 2 vols. London, 1927, 1928.

Ornsby, G., *York: diocesan histories.* London, no date.

Phillott, H. W., *Hereford: diocesan histories.* London, no date.

Processional of the nuns of Chester, edited by J. W. Legg. Henry Bradshaw Society Pub. vol. 18. London, 1899.

Processionale ad usum . . . Sarum, edited by W. G. Henderson. Leeds, 1882.

Prymer, edited by H. Littlehales. Early English Text Society, original series 105, 109. London, 1895, 1897.

Rock, D., *Church of our fathers as seen in St. Osmund's rite for the cathedral of Salisbury,* 4 vols. Edited by G. W. Hart and W. H. Frere. London, 1903-1904.

Sarum Missal, edited by J. W. Legg. Oxford, 1916.

Sarum missal, done into English by A. H. Pearson. London, 1884. 2nd edition.

Sarum missal, translated by F. E. Warren. London, 1911. (Library of liturgiology and ecclesiology for English readers, vols. 8 and 9.)

S. Silviae, quae fertur, Peregrinatio ad loca sancta, CSEL 39. 35-101. Vindobonae, 1898.

Stroppel, R., *Liturgie und geistliche Dichtung 1050-1300.* Frankfort am Main, 1927.

Swete, H. B., *Church services and service books before the Reformation.* London, 1896.

Thalhofer, V. and Eisenhofer, L., *Handbuch der katholischen Liturgik,* 2 vols. Freiburg im Breisgau, 1912.

Tropary of Ethelred, published in *Missale . . . Eboracensis,* above.

Winchester troper, edited by W. H. Frere. Henry Bradshaw Society Pub. London, 1894.

Wordsworth, C., *Ceremonies and processions of the cathedral church of Salisbury.* Cambridge, 1901.

———, *Notes on mediaeval services in England.* London, 1898.

———, and H. Littlehales, *The old service books of the English church.* London, 1904.

York breviary, edited by J. H. Srawley. Surtees Society Pub. vols. 71, 75. Durham, 1880, 1883.

V. Hymns and Medieval Culture, especially Art, Drama, Literature and Music

Acta Sanctorum quotquot orbe coluntur . . . collegit Joannes Bollandus etc., 1643 *et seq.*

Addison, J. T., *Medieval Missionary.* A study of the conversion of northern Europe A. D. 500-1300. New York, 1936. This book supersedes earlier works.

Allen, P. S., *Romanesque lyric.* Chapel Hill, 1928.

Altamira, R., *History of Spanish Civilization,* translated by P. Volkov. London, 1930.

Ante-Nicene fathers, vol. VIII. American Reprint. Buffalo, 1886. For Apocryphal books of the N. T.

Antiphonale monasticum pro diurnis horis ordinis Sancti Benedicti a solesmensibus monachis restitutum. Parisiis, Tornaci, Romae. 1935. For Gregorian music.

Apocryphal New Testament, edited by M. R. James. Oxford, 1924.

Blume, C., "Hymnologie und Kulturgeschichte des Mittelalters", in *Festschrift f. Georg von Hertling.* Kempten, 1913. Pp. 117-130.

Brehier, L., *L'art chrétien.* Paris, 1928. 2nd edition.

Brown, C., *English lyrics of the 13th century.* London, 1932.

———, *Religious lyrics of the 14th century.* Oxford, 1924.

———, *Religious lyrics of the 15th century.* Oxford, 1939.

———, *Register of Middle English religious and didactic verse,* Pt. II. Oxford, 1920.

Burdach, K., *Vorspiel,* Bd. I. Über den Ursprung des mittelalterlichen Minnesangs, Liebesromans und Frauendienstes. Halle S., 1925.

Chambers, E. K., *Mediaeval Stage,* 2 vols. Oxford, 1903.

Clark, J. M., *The abbey of St. Gall as a center of literature and art.* Cambridge, 1926.

Cohen, G., *Histoire de la mise en scene dans le théatre religieux français du moyen age.* Paris, 1926. Fine bibliography.

Creizenach, W., *Geschichte des neueren Dramas,* vol. I. Halle, 1911.

Cutts, E. L., *Parish priests and their people in the Middle Ages.* London, 1914.

Delehaye, H., *Les legendes hagiographiques.* Bruxelles, 1905.

Diehl, C., *Manuel d'art Byzantin.* Paris, 1910.

Dill, S., *Roman Society in Gaul in the merovingian age.* London, 1926.

Douglas, W. C., *Church music in history and practice.* New York, 1937.

Drake, M. and W., *Saints and their emblems.* London, 1916.

Duchartre, P. L., *Mittelalterliche Plastik in Frankreich.* München, 1925.

Evans, J., *Monastic life at Cluny, 910-1157.* London, 1931.

Farmer, H. G., *Historical facts for the Arabian musical influence.* London, 1930.

———, *History of Arabian music to the XIIIth C.* London, 1929.

Fellerer, K. G., *Beiträge zur Musikgeschichte Freisings* etc. Freising, 1926.

Gams, Dom P. B., *Die Kirchengeschichte von Spanien,* 5 vols. Regensburg, 1862-1879.

Garcia Villada, *Historia eclesiástica de España,* 3 vols. in 5. Madrid, 1929-1936.

Gasquet, F. A., *Parish life in mediaeval England.* London, 1907.

Gautier, L., *La poésie religieuse dans les cloîtres des IXe - XIe siècles.* Paris, 1887.

Gougaud, L., *Les chrétientés Celtiques.* Paris, 1911.

Gourmont, R. de, *Le Latin mystique;* les poetes de l'antiphonaire et la symbolique au moyen âge. Paris, 1913.

Hauttmann, M., *Die Kunst des frühen Mittelalters.* Berlin, 1929.

Higginson, J. V., *Revival of Gregorian chant.* Papers of the Hymn Society of America, XV. New York, 1949.

Jacopo de Voragine, *Golden legend.* Lives of the saints as Englished by William Caxton, 7 vols. *Temple Classics,* edited by F. S. Ellis. London, 1900.

Jeanroy, A., *Le théatre religieux en France du XIe au XIIIe siècles.* Paris, 1924.

———, *Les origines de la poésie lyrique en France au moyen âge.* Paris, 1925.

Kretzman, P. E., *The liturgical element in the earliest forms of the medieval drama.* Un. of Minnesota Studies in Language and Literature, no. 4, 1916.

Künstle, K., *Ikonographie der Heiligen.* Freiburg im Breisgau, 1926.

Lang, P. H., *Music in western civilization.* New York, 1941.

Lévi-Provençal, E., *La civilization arabe en Espagne, vue general.* Le Caire, 1938.

Luchaire, A. (D.J.A.) *Social France at the time of Philip Augustus,* translated from the 2nd French edition by E. B. Krehbiel. New York, 1912.

Mâle, E., *L'art religieux du XIIe siècle en France.* Paris, 1922.

———, *L'art religieux du XIIIe siècle en France.* Paris, 1923.

———, *L'art religieux de la fin du moyen âge en France.* Paris, 1922.

———, *L'art allemand et l'art français du moyen âge.* Paris, 1922.

Meyer, K., *Selections from ancient Irish poetry.* London, 1911.

Meyer, W., *Gesammelte Abhandlungen zur mittellateinischen Rythmik,* 2 vols. in 1. Berlin, 1905.

Muller, H. F., "Pre-history of the mediaeval drama", *Zeitschrift für romanische Philologie,* Bd. 44 (1924) 544-575.

Nelson, P., *Ancient stained glass in England.* London, 1913.

Owst, G. R., *Preaching in medieval England.* Cambridge, 1926.

Prior, E. A. and Gardner, A., *An account of medieval figure-sculpture in England.* Cambridge, 1912.

Pokorny, J., *Die älteste Lyrik der grünen Insel.* Halle S., 1923.

Quasten, J., *Musik und Gesang in den Kulten der heidnischen Antike und christlichen Frühzeit.* Münster im W., 1930.

Raby, F. J. E., *A history of secular Latin poetry in the M. A.*, 2 vols. Oxford, 1934.

Riaño, J. F., *Critical and bibliographical notes on early Spanish music.* London, 1887.

Schroeder, Sister M. J., *Mary-Verse in Meistergesang.* Washington, D. C., 1942.

Sedgwick, W. B., "Origin of rhyme", *Revue Bénédictine*, 36 (1924) 330-346.

Singer, S., *Die Dichterschule von St. Gallen.* Leipzig, 1922.

Spanke, H., *Deutsche und französische Dichtung des Mittelalters.* Stuttgart, 1943.

———, "Zur Geschichte der spanischen Musik des Mittelalters", *Hist. Vierteljahrschrift*, 28 (1934), 737-66.

Steinen, W. von den, *Notker der Dichter und seine geistliche Welt*, 2 vols., Bern, 1948. Reviews and supersedes earlier literature on Notker. Vol. II contains complete works of Notker.

Strzygowski, J., *Origin of Christian church art*, translated by Dalton and Braunholtz. Oxford, 1923.

Taylor, H. O., *The medieval mind*, 2 vols. New York, 1914.

Trend, J. B., *The music of Spanish history to 1600.* London, 1926.

Turner, W., "Irish teachers in the Carolingian revival of learning", *Cath. Un. Bulletin*, XIII, Washington, D. C., 1907, pp. 382, 562.

Van Doren, Dom R., *Étude sur l'influence musicale de l'abbaye de Saint-Gall.* Louvain, 1925.

Wagner, P., *Einführung in die Gregorianischen Melodien*, London, 1907.

———, "Morgen-und Abendland in der Musikgeschichte", *Stimmen der Zeit*, Bd. 114 (1927) 131-145.

———, "Der mozarabische Kirchengesang und seiner Überlieferung", in Finke, H., *Gesammelte Aufsätze zur Kulturgeschichte Spaniens*, Reihe I, Bd. I, p. 102-141. Münster, 1928.

Ward, J. B., *Gregorian Chant II.* Belgium, 1949.

Wehrle, W. O., *The macaronic hymn tradition in medieval English literature.* Washington, D. C., 1933.

Wells, J. E., *Manual of the writings in middle English 1050-1400.* New Haven, 1916.

Von Winterfeld, P., "Die Dichterschule St. Gallens und der Reichenau unter der Karolingern und Ottonen", "Stilfragen der lateinischen Dichtung des Mittelalters", *Deutsche Dichter*, p. 402-422, 423-444. München, 1922.

Woerdeman, Dom J., "The source of the Easter play", *Orate Fratres*, 20 (1946), Apr. 25, p. 262-272.

Young, K., *The drama of the medieval church*, 2 vols. Oxford, 1933.

Ruth Ellis Messenger

Publications

Ethical Teachings in the Latin Hymns of Medieval England, Columbia Un. Studies in History, Economics and Public Law (New York, 1930) 210 p.

Articles

Papers of the Hymn Society of America, Editor, Carl F. Price, New York.

No. III, "The Praise of the Virgin in Early Latin Hymns," 1932, reprinted 1944, 10 p.

No. IX, "Christian Hymns of the First Three Centuries," 1942, reprinted 1949, 25 p.

No. XIV, "Latin Hymns of the Middle Ages," 1948, 14 p.

Transactions and Proceedings of the American Philological Association

"Hymns and Sequences of the Sarum Use," vol. 59 (1928) 99-129.

Abstract: "Origin of the Sequence," vol. 64 (1933) lxv-lxvi.

"The Descent Theme in Medieval Latin Hymns," vol. 67 (1936) 126-57.

"Whence the Ninth Century Hymnal?," vol. 69 (1938) 446-64.

"Recent Studies in Medieval Latin Hymns," vol. 71 (1940) 248-261.

"The Mozarabic Hymnal," vol. 75 (1944) 103-126.

"Salve Festa Dies," vol. 78 (1947) 208-222.

"Medieval Processional Hymns before 1100," vol. 80 (1949) 375-392.

"Processional Hymns of the Later Middle Ages," vol. 81 (1950) 185-199.

Miscellaneous articles

Catholic Choirmaster

"Notker Balbulus," Sept. 1946, 101-5, 139.

"Sancta Maria quid est?," June, 1950, 59-61, 81.

"Rabanus Maurus," Summer, 1951, 55-57.

Classical Outlook

"Medieval Easter Hymns," April, 1944, 65-6.

"Adam of St. Victor," Feb., 1947, 49-51.

"Greek Hymns of the Nativity," Dec., 1948, 25-6.

"The Eighth Day," May, 1950, 88-9.

Classical Weekly

"The Legend of St. Agnes in Early Latin Hymns," Nov. 29, 1943, 75.

"The Legend of St. Eulalia in Mozarabic Hymns," Oct. 9, 1944, 12-3.

"Hymns in the Horae Eboracenses," Jan. 15, 1945, 90-5.

Folia

"Sources of the Sequence Scalam ad Caelos," May, 1947, 55-63.

"Classical Influence in the Hymns of St. Ambrose," vol. 4, nos. 1-3 (1949) 1-5.

"Aurelius Prudentius Clemens," vol. 6, no. 2 (1952) 78-99.

The Hymn

"John Mason Neale, Translator," Oct., 1951, 5-10.

Speculum

"Hymnista," Jan., 1947, 83-4.

Traditio

"Mozarabic Hymns in Relation to Contemporary Culture in Spain," vol. 4 (1946) 149-77.

Index

Index of Latin Hymns

General Index